M000268369

Hearts of Gold

MEDICAL COLLEGE OF GEORGIA
CHILDREN'S MEDICAL CENTER

Designed, Edited, and Manufactured by
Favorite Recipes® Press
an imprint of

FRP™

P.O. Box 305142
Nashville, Tennessee 37230
1-800-358-0560

Book Design: Sara Anglin
Project Manager: Judy Jackson
Art Director: Steve Newman

Library of Congress Number: 97-74951
ISBN: 0-9659707-0-1
First Printing: 1997
7,000 copies

We are extremely grateful to our sponsors, who believed
in our efforts. We are proud to acknowledge and support
BellSouth, Bi-Lo, Guidant CPI, NationsBank, Natural Artesian
Springs Water and Pacesetter.

The children in this book were photographed by Tim
Conway, who has graciously shared his talents with us and
brings to you the best of our children being children. Many
of the children in these photographs have special hearts—
transplants, valve replacements or surgical repairs to help
complex, life-threatening problems.

We gratefully acknowledge the authors of the inspirational
messages used throughout this book. These favorite and
personal messages were compiled by parents and friends
of the Children's Heart Program Volunteer Council at the
Medical College of Georgia Children's Medical Center.
Although many of the sources are unknown to the compilers,
their words have been uplifting and instrumental in helping
us meet our daily challenges, especially during the most
difficult times. We regret if anyone is not properly recognized.

Proceeds from the sale of *Hearts of Gold* will go toward
projects and activities benefiting children with heart
disease and their families at the Medical College of
Georgia Children's Medical Center in Augusta, Georgia.
To order additional copies, call the Medical College of
Georgia Children's Heart Program Volunteer Council at
706-721-COOK.

About the Cover: Dr. William B. Strong, Chief, Section of
Pediatric Cardiology, is serving our children with special
hearts, a reflection of his dedication throughout his career.

$\mathcal{D}$EDICATION

---

*It is with great pride that we dedicate this book to the children
with special hearts who boldly paved the way, and to our
children who continue to inspire our lives as they meet the
challenges of childhood heart disease.*

$\mathscr{F}$OREWORD

What makes a cookbook distinctive? Down-home recipes that have stood the test of time generation after generation? Recipes exotic enough to impress even the most discriminating dinner guests? Healthy recipes to keep up with the latest nutritional guidelines?

This cookbook is filled with all of the above. But the most distinctive feature of this book is that it nourishes not only the body but the soul. Its contributors are people whose lives are touched daily by children with imperfect hearts. Yes, these children have heart defects, some severe enough to make every day of their lives on earth a miracle. But God seems to have compensated for these defects by infusing these children's hearts with enough joy to transcend any obstacle. Their spirit is the inspiration for *Hearts of Gold.*

The health care professionals who help mend our children's faulty but full hearts, the parents who have learned to live one day at a time, the friends and family members who bolster sagging spirits, the volunteers who generously give of their time and talent to help sick children . . . these are the people who have compiled *Hearts of Gold.* These people know that once you are enveloped by a desperately ill child, your life is never again the same. Children are naturally joyous and optimistic, even in the face of medical challenges. They teach us all that every moment is a blessing and a treasure.

How can you capture that spirit in a cookbook? This book not only features the most delicious recipes ever, but serves as a reminder that optimism, faith and courage can help us live life to its fullest, even in the face of great obstacles. Every individual deserves to lead a long and full life and our children with special hearts are no exception. Inspirational thoughts and quotes are interspersed throughout the book. These favorite thoughts have provided inspiration, faith and hope during the daily challenges of parenting a child with heart disease. Many families have found comfort in these words as our children undergo heart surgery with the hope of creating a more perfect heart. Even if you've never known a child with a heart defect, the wisdom and inspiration found within these pages will offer strength and encouragement to face life's challenges.

From the bottom of my heart, thank you for supporting our special children by investing in *Hearts of Gold.* Because of you, the Children's Heart Program Volunteer Council at the Medical College of Georgia Children's Medical Center can continue to invest in programs and projects designed for children with heart disease. And as the mother of a little boy who has undergone nine heart surgeries and who has lived with the daily challenges associated with heart disease, I know what your support means to these children and their families. Thank you for having a Heart of Gold.

—Daniel's Mommy

Contents

PREFACE

Imagine 90 doctors preparing their favorite culinary delights for 700 guests. Add community sponsors, countless volunteers, and a most important cause—children with heart disease. This is the recipe for Doctors Who Cook, the annual fund raiser sponsored by the Children's Heart Program Volunteer Council at the Medical College of Georgia Children's Medical Center.

Many of the recipes in this collection have been submitted by Doctors Who Cook participants and are easily recognized by the chef's hat emblem beside the recipe. Other recipes are favorites of family and friends of children with special hearts.

The recipes in our Young at Heart chapter were submitted by children with heart disease and their siblings. These recipes can be prepared by children with adult supervision. In addition, on page 184, we have included a nutritional profile of some of the more heart-healthy recipes. We are proud to present to you *Hearts of Gold–A Collection of Recipes from Doctors Who Cook and Friends of the Children's Heart Program*.

The proceeds from *Hearts of Gold* will help us continue to fund projects benefiting pediatric cardiac patients at the Medical College of Georgia Children's Medical Center. Our projects are individualized because each child's needs are different. Some of our projects have included providing transportation so a child can attend a clinic visit to receive medical care, issuing Life Alert bracelets that provide information in case of a medical emergency, coordinating all-expenses-paid family vacations for children with life-threatening heart disease, coordinating "Happy Hearts Family Fun Day" reunions for children and their families and the medical personnel who saved their lives, producing *Beat-by-Beat*, the educational and inspirational newsletter for parents and hosting informational parents' forums. Additionally, the family support service we provide during a child's hospitalization is the backbone of our volunteer efforts.

The Heart and Soul of Our Program . . . Volunteers

We've been there—right where hundreds of other families sit as their child is undergoing open-heart surgery. We have looked out the same window as other families, watching as the world busily continues on unaware of how critical the next few hours or days are to a child with heart disease. We know firsthand what parents and families go through during a child's heart surgery and recuperation. The challenges are great when a child and his family must devote their lives to continuous medical care but there is a unique healing in helping others who are going through similar experiences.

The Children's Heart Program Volunteer Council at the Medical College of Georgia Children's Medical Center understands the need to give hope and comfort to others based on our own experience. The council was established by parents and friends of children with imperfect hearts to identify and implement projects that directly benefit these special children and their families. In just a few short months, the council grew to include community leaders, hospital staff and parents of healthy children because they couldn't imagine what life would be like raising a critically ill child and wanted to help make life a little easier for these special children.

The volunteer council has come a long way since 1995 when Dr. William Strong, Chief, Section of Pediatric Cardiology at the Medical College of Georgia, first encouraged us to think about the feasibility of beginning a volunteer organization to benefit these children. After learning about courage and strength from our children who have undergone open-heart surgeries, we knew this was going to be a way of life from then on. Many of us have stood beside their hospital beds not knowing how to make things better—the Children's Heart Program Volunteer Council fulfills this need as we help other parents who also had that same terrible feeling of helplessness. This core group of volunteers has since grown into a vital part of the Children's Heart Program at the Medical College of Georgia Children's Medical Center. The volunteer council was organized to identify and implement activities and programs for the Children's Heart Program, emphasizing family support, community awareness and financial development. We also support the projects of the MCG Children's Heart Program, consisting of the Children's Heart Group, the Cardiovascular Studies Group and the Heart Development Group. The volunteer council meets regularly to carry out our goals which, very simply, are mandated by the needs of the children and their families.

A Tradition of Caring

It was more than a century ago when 10-year-old Sadie Campbell went with her mother to the hospital to visit a crippled child named Hetty. Young Sadie was concerned because Hetty was on a ward with adults—there was no special wing for children. At her birthday party, Sadie asked her friends to bring a dime to help hospitalized children instead of a present. Sadie sent 12 dimes to the Hospital Association in Augusta, Georgia, to help improve the condition of hospital facilities. The Hospital Association was a group of women who set out to make improvements to City Hospital. The directors were so impressed with Sadie's efforts that they voted to add $37.50, the balance of money raised for a maternity ward, to her donation.

Thus, the Children's Ward Fund was created. While these funds were earmarked to add a children's ward to City Hospital, the Hospital Association became impatient and the idea of the children's ward grew into that of a separate hospital for children.

This group of women on the Hospital Association formed a separate and distinct Children's Hospital Association. They would work closely with the parent organization, the Hospital Association. During the years that followed, the creation of the new children's hospital was delayed due to lack of funds despite the huge efforts of the Children's Hospital Association's President, Mrs. Mary G. Cumming. However, in 1910, the generosity of Mrs. Grace Shaw Duff of New York City allowed the first dedicated children's hospital to become a reality. It was during a regular visit to Augusta that her husband became ill and died.

Mrs. Duff appreciated the kind treatment she had received in Augusta during her husband's illness. After learning about Mrs. Cumming's efforts to build a new children's hospital, Mrs. Duff donated $25,000 to the hospital fund as a memorial to her husband. This donation enabled a hospital to be constructed for children—the first in Georgia and the South. She named the hospital The Wilhenford, after her husband, William, her father, Henry, and her son, Bradford.

The Wilhenford Hospital for Children successfully operated until 1941. The building became the property of the Medical College of Georgia, the state's health sciences university, and was demolished in 1959.

The Georgia General Assembly approved funds in 1993 for the Medical College of Georgia to construct a new children's hospital. Ironically, the new Children's Medical Center is located just a few hundred yards from where the Wilhenford Children's Hospital once stood.

Today, the Medical College of Georgia Children's Medical Center provides comprehensive care to children of all ages. Pediatric specialists representing every field of medicine work in concert with general pediatricians to practice, teach and discover the most current approaches to health care for children.

Pediatric specialists, including anesthesiologists, cardiologists, cardiothoracic surgeons, oncologists, neurologists, ophthalmologists and many others, are dedicated to the immediate health care needs of children and to the future of pediatric medicine. The Children's Medical Center is a family-centered care facility that has relied on the personal hospital experiences of its Family Advisory Council members and the Children's Advisory Council members in all design phases of the new hospital. The 220,000-square-foot hospital includes 88 medical/surgical beds, a 16-bed pediatric intensive care unit and a 36-bed neonatal intensive care unit. The state-of-the-art facility features a reflecting pool, a large video aquarium, an outdoor garden and an expanded Family Resource Center.

People like Sadie Campbell, who recognized that sick children needed a special place, Mrs. Grace Shaw Duff, who kindly provided the financial support for a children's hospital, and Mrs. Mary Cumming, who persevered until the hospital became a reality, truly had hearts of gold. Their vision continues through the work of individuals today who provide innovative care for children.

$\mathscr{A}$CKNOWLEDGEMENTS

We wish to express our warmest thanks to those who shared ideas and all-time favorites for *Hearts of Gold*. The recipes in this collection have been individually tested and represent only a portion of the recipes submitted for consideration. Due to lack of space and similarities in recipes, all could not be printed in this book. After collecting and testing the recipes, we believe they reflect a general sampling of favorites. It is our hope that you enjoy preparing them for your family and friends as we have for ours.

Executive Cookbook Committee

Betts Murdison, chairman
Mindy Mets, co-chairman
Marisa Levy, recipe chairman
Bunny Garcia
Gloria Ginn
Marilyn Levy
Julie Ginn Moretz

Cookbook Panel

Tracye Cohen
Christine Hurley-Deriso
Becky Dietz
Karen Duval
Judy English
Helen Ferguson
Eva Foreman
Audrey Gelbart
Rhonda Graybeal
Bonnie Hadden
Sherry B. Hajec
Pat Harrell
Jim Leibach
Cindy McNeill
Cindy Miller
Pam Mills
Bonnie Owen
Katherine Price
Ann Rogers
Sally Rogers
Derindia Shapiro
Vivian Slotin
Karen Steinhart
JoAnn Temples
Pam Weinberger

Children Pictured

Blake Norris
Daniel Moretz
Brittany Furman
Jillian Owen
Chandler Moody
Alex Levy
Joey Mets
Steven Mets
Sean Levy
Baillie Conway
Michael Poda
Austin McNeill
Becca Moon
Ian Owen
Dylan McNeill
Frank Johnson
Ebonnée Johnson
Patrick Garcia
Scott Murdison
Todd Garcia
Geordie Murdison
Miller Price
Callie Sullivan
Joshua Anderson
Zachary Anderson

Contributors List

Dr. Andy Allgood
Holly Anderson
Dr. and Mrs. Matthew Bachinski
Lynne Barber
Dr. Deborah Bates
Drs. Jose and Lynnette Bauza
Dr. Suzi Domel-Baxter
Dr. Sharon P. Beall
Donna Beard
Dr. and Mrs. Jack Benjamin
Dr. James W. Bennett
Dr. and Mrs. Wayne Beveridge
Dr. Lynne Brannen
Dr. David Brantley
Dr. Steve Brooks
Dr. Spence Brudno
Barbara Bush
Debbie Byrd
Sylvia Campbell
Dr. Ralph Caruana
Florinda Canizares Chun
Adria Clark
Vickie Clark
Hillary Rodham Clinton
Dr. Lynne Coule
Dr. Frederick Cox
Connie Crenshaw
Dean Crumbley
Joan Cundey
Cindy Daniel

Drs. Gisela Mercado-Deane and
    Daniel A. Deane
Dr. Celia P. Dunn
Renita G. Durant
Sharon Faircloth
Hankie Fishback
Dr. and Mrs. Gene Fisher
Kenneth Luke Fisher
Dr. Margaret H. Fitch
Anne Fulcher
Dr. Michael Fulford
Bunny Garcia
Audrey Gelbart
Gloria Ginn
Dr. Kevin Grigsby
Bonnie Hadden
Allison Lee Hajec
Sherry B. Hajec
Lois Hanson
Maureen Hardy
Dr. and Mrs. Herbert S. Harper
Pat Harrell
Anna Hatcher
Nan Hausman
Donna Hillmon
Dr. Les Hixon
Becky Hollins
Matti Holt
Dr. Tom Howdieshell
Dr. and Mrs. Tom Huff

Dr. Robert Introna
Dr. and Mrs. John Ivanhoe
Dr. Kevin Ivey
Betty Jenkins
Miriam Jenkins
Dr. Carol Joriman
Dr. Sharon Kaminer
Dr. and Mrs. William Kanto
Dr. Gary Katcoff
Charlotte Daniel Keeble
Dr. T. Scott Key
Charlotte Klein
Dr. Kent Kronowski
Dr. Linda Leatherberry
Dr. Mark Lee
Dr. Carol A. Lefebvre
Celinda M. Levine
Marilyn Levy
Marisa Levy
Dr. Charles W. Linder
Geriann C. Lioi
Yolanda Yvetta Livingston
Dr. Robert E. Lofgren
Dr. Josephine Lopez
Carla Love
Lucy Lowery
Dr. William Lutin
Sushila K. Mahesh
Dr. and Mrs. Arlie Mansberger
Dr. Jim Marek

continued on page 12

Sandy Marek
Susan Z. Marks
Dr. Michael McBee
Susie McConnell
Dr. Kathleen McKie
Rebecca D. McKie
Dr. Virgil C. McKie
Austin McNeill
Dr. and Mrs. Browning McRee
Mindy Mets
Mary Montgomery
Mark and Mandy Moody
Dr. and Mrs. Victor Moore
Daniel Joseph Ginn Moretz
David L. Moretz
Julie Ginn Moretz
Rose Moseley
Wanda Mundy
Betts Murdison
Dr. Ken Murdison
Dr. and Mrs. David Myers
Dr. and Mrs. Steven Nelson
Heidi Nelson
Betsy Nunamaker
Tevis Olliff
Marcy Oppenheimer
Elizabeth J. Ostric
Bonnie Owen
Ian Owen
Dr. Robert Parrish

Jan Parsons
Wendy Paschal
Andy Philipp
Gabrielle Philipp
Michael Poda
Steve Poe
Dr. and Mrs. J. Nicholas Powell
Dr. Ned and Ellen Pruitt
Dr. and Mrs. Cliff Reeber
Dr. David Reid
Ann Rogers
Dr. Laura Rogers
Kathy Rosenblum
Dr. Joe and Edie Rubin
Deborah Satchell
Michelle Scharite
Jillian Schilling
Terry Schilling
Michelle Shackford
Derindia Shapiro
Dr. Sarita B. Sharma
Dr. Michael K. Shrout
Marlene Sides
Susan Simmons
Vivian Slotin
Annette C. Smart
Drs. John and Suzanne Smith
Dr. L. W. Smith III
Dr. Tito Sobrinho
Patricia Sodomka

Benjamin Stalvey
Tracie Stalvey
Dr. Curt M. Steinhart
Karen Steinhart
Dr. Joseph M. Still, Jr.
Patti Stinson
Dr. Victoria Stoeppler
Dr. William Strong
Dr. Elizabeth Sunde
Dr. and Mrs. J. B. Tanenbaum
JoAnn Temples
Tiffany Temples
Dr. Fred Thielke
Dr. and Mrs. Barrett Trotter
Dr. Edward Truemper
Cindy Tuttle
Dr. Warren Umansky
Ann Utz
Janet Vincent
Laura Anne Waterman
Janet Weinberger
Dr. Christopher Welch
Erma White
Gina Wilkie
Dr. Mark Williams
Patty Williams
Ruth Wilson
Susan Wise
Dr. Betty Wray
Dr. Lionel Zumbro

Light-Hearted

*A*PPETIZERS AND *B*EVERAGES

"Friendship . . . is the golden thread that ties the heart of all the world." –*John Evelyn*

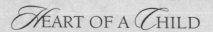 HEART OF A CHILD

Whatever you write on the heart of a child,
No waters can wash away,
The sands may be shifted when billows are wild
And the effects of time may decay.
Some stories may perish, some songs to be forgot.
But this engraven record, time changes it not.

Whatever you write on the heart of a child,
A story of gladness or care
That heaven has blessed or earth defiled,
Will linger unchangeably there.

ANTIPASTO

1½ cups vegetable oil

1 cup vinegar

1 small onion, finely chopped

1½ teaspoons chopped garlic

2 teaspoons crushed peppercorns

1 teaspoon crushed rosemary
    leaves

1 teaspoon basil

1 teaspoon oregano

⅛ teaspoon salt, or to taste

Green bell peppers, cauliflower,
    carrots, green olives, celery
    and hot peppers, cut into
    bite-size pieces

Swiss cheese, Cheddar cheese and
    hot pepper cheese, cut into cubes

Pepperoni slices

Cucumbers and tomatoes,
    cut into bite-size pieces

Combine the oil, vinegar, onion, garlic, peppercorns, rosemary, basil, oregano and salt in a medium bowl and mix well. Combine the green peppers, cauliflower, carrots, olives, celery, hot peppers, cheese and pepperoni in a large bowl. Add the vinegar mixture and mix well. Marinate in the refrigerator for 12 to 24 hours. Add the cucumbers during the last 4 hours of marinating; add the tomatoes 1 hour before serving time.

Yield: 6 to 8 servings

BRIE BAKED IN PUFF PASTRY

1 sheet puff pastry, thawed
1 small round of Brie, rind removed
1/2 to 3/4 cup apricot preserves
1 egg, beaten

Roll the pastry into a piece large enough to envelop the Brie. Spread the top and side of the Brie with the preserves. Position in the center of the pastry. Fold the pastry over the cheese. Brush the edges with part of the egg to seal. Place the Brie right side up in an ovenproof dish. Brush with the remaining egg. Chill for 30 minutes. Preheat the oven to 425 degrees. Bake for 15 to 20 minutes or until the pastry is golden brown. Serve with crackers or apple slices.

Yield: 8 to 10 servings

BRAISED CELERY WITH TOASTED ALMONDS

1 1/2 cups chicken broth
3 1/2 cups sliced celery
1 1/2 tablespoons butter or
*   margarine, softened*
1/4 cup flour
1 egg yolk
2 tablespoons half-and-half
1/8 teaspoon white pepper, or
*   to taste*
1/3 cup toasted slivered almonds

Bring the chicken broth to a boil in a medium saucepan. Add the celery. Simmer, covered, for 5 minutes or until the celery is tender-crisp. Remove the celery to a warm serving bowl. Blend the butter and flour together. Add to the cooking liquid. Cook for 1 minute, stirring constantly. Stir in a mixture of the egg yolk, half-and-half and pepper. Cook over low heat for 2 to 3 minutes or until thickened, adding additional flour if needed. Spoon over the celery. Sprinkle with the almonds.

Yield: 4 to 6 servings

Delta Cheese Rolls

1 pound extra-sharp Cheddar
   cheese, shredded
1/3 cup mayonnaise
2 tablespoons milk
1 tablespoon dried parsley
6 green onions, finely chopped
1 tablespoon Worcestershire sauce
1/2 teaspoon Tabasco sauce
1/2 teaspoon onion powder
1/2 teaspoon garlic powder
1/2 teaspoon black pepper
1/2 teaspoon cayenne
1 loaf sliced white bread, crusts
   trimmed
1/2 cup melted unsalted butter

Preheat the oven to 375 degrees. Combine the cheese, mayonnaise, milk, parsley, green onions, Worcestershire sauce, Tabasco sauce, onion powder, garlic powder, black pepper and cayenne in a bowl and mix well. Flatten 1 bread slice with a rolling pin. Spread with some of the cheese mixture. Roll up the bread diagonally; secure with a wooden pick. Repeat with the remaining bread and cheese mixture. Place the rolls on a baking sheet. Brush with the butter. Bake for 10 to 12 minutes or until the cheese melts and the bread is golden brown.

Yield: 8 to 10 servings

Mom's Chicken Wings

1 teaspoon salt
1 teaspoon white pepper
1 teaspoon garlic powder
1/2 cup melted margarine or butter
1 pound chicken drumettes

Preheat the oven to 350 degrees. Dissolve the salt, pepper and garlic powder in the margarine in a bowl. Dip the chicken into the mixture. Place in a foil-lined baking pan. Bake for 1 1/2 to 2 hours or until the chicken is crispy and cooked through. May add cinnamon, soy sauce or hot sauce to the melted margarine.

Yield: 4 servings

Buffalo Wings

Vegetable oil
36 chicken wings, disjointed
1/4 to 1/2 cup margarine
6 to 8 ounces hot sauce
   (not Tabasco sauce)
Chili powder to taste
Pepper to taste

Bring the oil to a brisk boil in a large skillet or deep fryer. Add the chicken. Fry until cooked through and almost crispy; drain well. Melt the margarine in a saucepan. Add the hot sauce and mix well. Cook until heated through; do not boil. Season generously with chili powder and pepper. Cook over medium heat until of desired consistency, stirring constantly. Dip the chicken into the sauce before serving. Serve with bleu cheese dressing and celery sticks.

Yield: 6 servings

Some people come into our lives and quickly go. Some stay for a while and leave footprints on our heart and we are never, ever the same.

—Unknown

Heavenly Chocolate Amaretto Tarts

66 vanilla wafers

2 cups flaked coconut

1 cup pecan pieces

1 cup melted butter or margarine

1 ounce unsweetened chocolate

1/2 cup butter, softened

2 cups confectioners' sugar

1 tablespoon vanilla extract

1/8 teaspoon salt, or to taste

4 egg yolks

3 tablespoons amaretto

1 1/2 cups whipping cream

1 1/2 tablespoons amaretto

Preheat the oven to 375 degrees. Crumble half the vanilla wafers in a food processor container. Add 1 cup of the coconut. Process for 5 seconds. Add 1/2 cup pecans. Process until mixed. Remove to a large bowl. Repeat the process with the remaining vanilla wafers, coconut and pecans. Pour 1 cup butter over the pecan mixture, tossing lightly until well mixed. Fill each miniature muffin cup with 1 tablespoon of the mixture. Press to form a crust over the bottom and side of the muffin cups. Bake for 8 to 10 minutes or until brown. Let cool. Loosen the tart shells from the side of the muffin cups. Melt the chocolate in a saucepan over low heat; set aside. Beat 1/2 cup butter in a mixer bowl. Add the confectioners' sugar gradually, beating constantly at medium speed until smooth. Add the chocolate, mixing until blended.

Stir in the vanilla extract and salt. Beat in the egg yolks 1 at a time. Add 3 tablespoons amaretto 1 tablespoon at a time, beating well after each addition. Beat the whipping cream in a mixer bowl until soft peaks form. Add 1 1/2 tablespoons amaretto gradually, mixing well after each addition. Fold 1 cup of the whipped cream into the chocolate mixture. Fill the tart shells with the chocolate mixture. Chill for 3 hours or until firm. Pipe or dollop the remaining whipped cream onto the tarts. Garnish with toasted sliced almonds.

Yield: 5 dozen

Cocktail Clam Puffs

1 cup clam broth
1/2 cup butter
1 cup flour
5 eggs, at room temperature
1/2 teaspoon milk
Clam Filling or Shrimp Filling

Preheat the oven to 400 degrees. Heat the clam broth in a saucepan over low heat. Add the butter. Bring to a boil. Add the flour all at once, stirring vigorously with a wooden spoon until the mixture leaves the side of the pan and forms a smooth ball. Place in a bowl. Add 4 eggs 1 at a time, beating well after each addition until a thick dough forms. Drop by level teaspoonfuls 1 inch apart onto a lightly greased baking sheet. Beat the remaining egg with the milk in a bowl. Brush over the tops of the dough. Bake at 400 degrees for 10 minutes. Reduce the oven temperature to 300 degrees. Bake for 20 to 25 minutes or until brown. Do not open the oven door while baking.

Remove the clam puffs from the oven and cool completely. Cut into halves horizontally. Fill with Clam Filling or Shrimp Filling and replace the tops. Place on a lightly greased baking sheet. May be frozen at this point; store in freezer bags. Bake at 400 degrees for 15 minutes. May replace 1 cup clam broth with the liquid from one 10-ounce can of clams mixed with enough water to measure 1 cup.

Yield: 6 dozen

Clam Filling

3 (10-ounce) cans minced clams,
   drained
16 ounces cream cheese with chives,
   softened
6 drops of Tabasco sauce, or to taste
1 teaspoon salt or seasoned salt
1/2 teaspoon pepper

Mix the clams, cream cheese, Tabasco sauce, salt and pepper in a bowl.

Shrimp Filling

2 (4-ounce) cans tiny shrimp,
   drained
2/3 cup toasted slivered almonds
1/2 cup finely chopped celery
2/3 cup sour cream
2 tablespoons finely chopped onion
1 teaspoon prepared mustard
1/4 teaspoon pepper

Mix the shrimp, almonds, celery, sour cream, onion, mustard and pepper in a bowl. Store the filling in the refrigerator if not using immediately.

You must give time to your fellow men—even if it's a little thing, do something for others— something for which you get no pay but the privilege of doing it.

—Albert Schweitzer

Empanadas

1 (10-ounce) package frozen patty
  shells, thawed
8 ounces ground beef
1/4 cup minced onion
3 tablespoons raisins
3 tablespoons chopped black olives
3 tablespoons tomato-based
  chili sauce
1 teaspoon chili powder
1/2 teaspoon ground cumin
1/2 teaspoon garlic salt
1/2 teaspoon ground coriander
Salt and pepper to taste

Preheat the oven to 400 degrees. Overlap the patty shells slightly on a lightly floured board. Roll 1/16 to 1/8 inch thick. Cut into rounds with a 3 1/2-inch cookie cutter. Brown the ground beef in a skillet over medium heat, stirring until crumbly. Add the onion. Cook until the onion is tender; drain well. Stir in the raisins, olives and chili sauce. Add the chili powder, cumin, garlic salt and coriander and mix well. Season with salt and pepper. Place 1 slightly rounded teaspoon of filling on each pastry round. Fold each in half and moisten the edges with water. Press together with a fork to seal. Reroll pastry scraps and repeat the filling procedure. Place 1 inch apart on nonstick baking sheets. Prick the tops with a fork. Bake for 20 minutes or until golden brown. Serve hot. Freezes well. Reheat frozen empanadas in a 400-degree oven for 7 to 8 minutes.

Yield: 2 dozen

Pecan-Stuffed Mushrooms

1 pound large fresh mushrooms
1/2 cup butter or margarine
1 clove of garlic, minced
1/2 cup chopped pecans
1/2 cup fine bread crumbs
1/2 teaspoon salt
1/4 teaspoon ground thyme
1/4 teaspoon pepper

Preheat the oven to 350 degrees. Rinse the mushrooms and pat dry. Remove and chop the stems. Place the caps in a buttered shallow baking dish. Melt the butter in a skillet. Add the mushroom stems and garlic. Sauté until tender. Add the pecans, bread crumbs, salt, thyme and pepper and mix well. Spoon into the mushroom caps. Bake for 15 minutes. Serve warm. May be served as a side dish with steak or London broil.

Yield: 2 dozen

Spicy Shrimp

1 pound shrimp
1/2 cup olive oil
2 tablespoons Old Bay seasoning
2 tablespoons lemon juice
1 teaspoon dried dill
2 tablespoons dried parsley
1 tablespoon honey
1 tablespoon soy sauce
1/8 teaspoon cayenne

Peel and devein the shrimp, leaving the tails intact. Place the shrimp in a shallow pan. Mix the oil, Old Bay seasoning, lemon juice, dill, parsley, honey, soy sauce and cayenne in a bowl. Pour over the shrimp. Marinate in the refrigerator for 1 hour. Preheat the oven to Broil. Drain the shrimp, discarding the marinade. Place the shrimp on a broiler pan. Broil for 4 to 5 minutes or until brown.

Yield: 3 to 4 servings

Shrimp Sea Island

5 pounds medium shrimp
5 medium Vidalia onions, thinly
    sliced, or other mild onions
2 cups olive oil
1 1/2 cups cider vinegar
1 large bottle capers
3/4 cup sugar
1/4 cup Worcestershire sauce
1/2 to 1 teaspoon Tabasco sauce
1 teaspoon salt

Boil the shrimp in water to cover in a saucepan for 3 minutes; drain immediately. Peel, devein and rinse the shrimp; drain well. Alternate layers of the shrimp and onions in a deep baking pan. Mix the oil, vinegar, undrained capers, sugar, Worcestershire sauce, Tabasco sauce and salt in a bowl. Pour over the shrimp and onions. Chill, covered, for 12 hours or longer, stirring occasionally. Drain well, discarding the marinade. Spoon the shrimp and onions into a glass bowl or onto a large lettuce-lined platter. Any leftover onions may be mixed with mayonnaise to serve as an hors d'oeuvre with saltines.

Yield: 5 pounds

Shrimp and Crab Rolls

1/2 cup drained canned water
    chestnuts

8 ounces lump crab meat, flaked

1 pound shrimp, shelled, rinsed

1 tablespoon minced peeled fresh
    gingerroot

1 1/2 tablespoons rice wine or Scotch

1 teaspoon salt

1 egg white, lightly beaten

1 1/2 teaspoons sesame oil

2 tablespoons cornstarch

24 frozen won ton wrappers,
    thawed

1 egg yolk

Corn oil

Blanch the water chestnuts in boiling water to cover in a small saucepan for 1 minute. Drain and refresh under cold water. Pat the water chestnuts dry and chop finely. Pat the crab meat dry. Purée the shrimp in a food processor until a smooth paste forms. Combine the shrimp, water chestnuts, crab meat, gingerroot, wine, salt, egg white and sesame oil in a bowl. Stir vigorously in 1 direction until well mixed. Stir in the cornstarch. Spoon into a pastry tube fitted with a plain 3/4-inch tip. Work with 6 won ton wrappers at a time, keeping the remaining wrappers covered with a dampened towel. Pipe a strip of the shrimp mixture down the center of each wrapper. Brush 1 edge of each wrapper with some of the egg yolk. Roll as for a jelly roll, pressing the brushed edge gently to seal; do not roll the wrappers too tightly or they will burst while cooking.

Heat 2 inches of corn oil to 350 degrees in a wok or deep fryer. Fry 6 rolls at a time in the hot oil for 1 1/2 to 2 minutes or until golden brown. Remove with tongs to paper towels to drain. Serve with plum sauce and Chinese hot mustard. The rolls may be prepared 1 day ahead and stored, loosely covered, in the refrigerator. To reheat, place on a rack in a shallow baking pan in a 350-degree oven. Heat for 10 minutes.

Yield: 2 dozen

Pizza on Rye

1 pound ground beef
1 pound hot sausage
1 pound Velveeta cheese, cut
   into cubes
2 teaspoons seasoned salt
2 teaspoons oregano
1 teaspoon minced garlic
2 teaspoons Worcestershire sauce
1 loaf party rye bread slices

Preheat the oven to Broil. Brown the ground beef and sausage in a skillet, stirring until crumbly; drain well. Add the cheese, seasoned salt, oregano, garlic and Worcestershire sauce and mix well. Cook over low heat until the cheese melts, stirring constantly. Spread on the bread slices. Place on a baking sheet. Broil until brown.

Yield: 20 servings

Florentine Artichoke Dip

1 (10-ounce) package frozen
   chopped spinach, thawed,
   drained
2 (6-ounce) jars marinated
   artichoke hearts, drained,
   chopped
3 cloves of garlic, minced
1/2 cup mayonnaise
12 ounces cream cheese, softened
2 tablespoons lemon juice
1 cup grated Parmesan cheese
1 1/2 cups fine dry bread crumbs

Preheat the oven to 375 degrees. Combine the spinach, artichoke hearts, garlic, mayonnaise, cream cheese, lemon juice and Parmesan cheese in a bowl and mix well. Spoon into a lightly greased 7x11-inch baking dish. Sprinkle with the bread crumbs. Bake for 25 minutes. Serve with crackers or breadsticks.

Yield: 4 cups

What lies behind us and what lies before us are tiny matters compared to what lies within us.

–Oliver Wendell Holmes

Cheese Balls

1 cup finely chopped pecans
16 ounces cream cheese, softened
1/4 cup minced bell pepper
1 (7-ounce) can crushed pineapple,
　　drained
1 teaspoon minced onion
1 teaspoon seasoned salt

Grind 1/2 cup of the pecans in a food processor and set aside. Combine the cream cheese, bell pepper, pineapple, onion, seasoned salt and remaining 1/2 cup pecans in a bowl and mix well. Chill for 40 to 45 minutes or until firm. Shape the mixture into 2 balls on waxed paper. Roll in the ground pecans. Serve with party crackers.

Yield: 20 to 30 servings

Cheese Spread

1 pound sharp Cheddar cheese,
　　shredded
1 cup mayonnaise
1 cup chopped pecans
1 small onion, finely chopped
4 teaspoons Worcestershire
　　sauce
Tabasco sauce to taste
Cayenne to taste

Mix the cheese, mayonnaise, pecans, onion, Worcestershire sauce, Tabasco sauce and cayenne in a bowl. Serve on party sandwiches or crackers.

Yield: 20 to 30 servings

I am only one, but still I am one; I cannot do everything, but still I can do something; and because I cannot do everything I will not refuse to do the something that I can do.

—Edward E. Hale

Caramel Fondue

1 (15-ounce) package caramels
1/2 cup whipping cream
2 tablespoons (or more) brandy
  or rum

Combine the caramels and whipping cream in a saucepan. Cook over low heat until the caramels melt, stirring occasionally. Stir in the brandy. Serve with apple wedges, large marshmallows, pineapple chunks and /or cherries for dipping. Recipe may be doubled.

Yield: 2 1/2 cups

Creamy Parmesan Fondue

16 ounces cream cheese or
  Neufchâtel cheese, softened
2 cups (about) milk
2 small cloves of garlic, minced, or
  1 teaspoon garlic salt
1 1/2 cups (about) grated
  Parmesan cheese
Salt to taste
Freshly ground pepper to taste, or
  thinly sliced green onions
1 (1-pound) loaf French bread,
  cut into 1-inch cubes

Place the cream cheese in a double boiler over simmering water. Stir in the milk gradually as the cream cheese melts, blending until smooth. Add the garlic and Parmesan cheese. Cook until the Parmesan cheese melts and the mixture is the correct consistency for dipping, stirring constantly; add additional milk if needed. Season with salt. Serve in a chafing dish over hot water or in a ceramic cheese fondue pot over a low alcohol flame. Sprinkle with pepper. Use the bread cubes for dipping.

Yield: 1 quart

Tex-Mex Nacho Dip

2 (10-ounce) cans jalapeño
   bean dip
3 medium avocados, peeled
2 tablespoons lemon juice
$^1/_2$ teaspoon salt
$^1/_4$ teaspoon pepper
1 cup sour cream
$^1/_2$ cup mayonnaise
1 envelope taco seasoning mix
1 large bunch green onions,
   chopped
3 medium tomatoes, chopped
2 (4-ounce) cans pitted black
   olives, chopped
8 ounces Cheddar cheese, shredded

Spread the bean dip in a shallow 9x13-inch glass dish. Mash the avocados with the lemon juice, salt and pepper in a bowl. Spread over the bean dip. Mix the sour cream, mayonnaise and taco seasoning mix in a bowl. Spread over the avocado mixture. Sprinkle with the green onions, tomatoes and olives. Cover with the cheese. Serve chilled with tortilla chips.

Yield: 15 to 18 servings

Green Apple Pesto

2 cups basil leaves, rinsed,
   dried
2 large Granny Smith apples,
   peeled, cored, cut into large
   chunks
$^3/_4$ cup grated Parmesan cheese
$^1/_2$ cup chopped walnuts
1 small clove of garlic, minced
$^1/_4$ teaspoon salt
$^1/_4$ cup extra-virgin olive oil

Combine the basil leaves, apples, cheese, walnuts, garlic and salt in a food processor. Process until mixed. Add the oil gradually with the food processor running, processing until smooth. Use as a dip or on turkey pita sandwiches.

Yield: 1$^3/_4$ cups

Salmon Dip

8 ounces cream cheese, softened
2 tablespoons chopped green
   onions
2 tablespoons catsup
2 tablespoons horseradish
1 (7-ounce) can salmon, drained,
   flaked

Combine the cream cheese, green onions, catsup and horseradish in a bowl and mix well. Stir in the salmon. Serve with crackers.

Yield: 20 to 25 servings

Smoked Salmon Ball

1 (16-ounce) can salmon, drained,
   flaked
8 ounces cream cheese, softened
1 tablespoon lemon juice
2 teaspoons grated onion
1/4 teaspoon liquid smoke
1 teaspoon horseradish
1/4 teaspoon salt
3 tablespoons chopped parsley
1/2 cup chopped pecans

Mix the salmon and cream cheese in a bowl. Add the lemon juice, onion, liquid smoke, horseradish and salt and mix well. Chill for several hours. Shape into a ball. Roll in a mixture of the parsley and pecans. Chill, loosely wrapped with waxed paper, until serving time. Serve with crackers.

Yield: 25 to 30 servings

Fresh Salsa Dip

2 (4-ounce) cans chopped black
   olives, drained
2 (4-ounces) cans chopped green
   chiles, drained
3 green onions, finely chopped
3 to 4 firm red tomatoes, finely
   chopped
2 to 3 tablespoons Italian salad
   dressing
2 tablespoons chopped fresh parsley

Mix the olives, green chiles, green onions, tomatoes and salad dressing in a bowl. Chill, covered, overnight. Top with the parsley. Serve with corn chips.

Yield: 20 to 25 servings

Zingy Pineapple Salsa

2 cups minced fresh or canned
   pineapple
2 medium cloves of garlic, minced
2 to 3 tablespoons minced fresh
   cilantro
2 tablespoons fresh lime juice
1/8 teaspoon salt
1/4 teaspoon cumin
Cayenne to taste

Combine the pineapple, garlic, cilantro, lime juice, salt, cumin and cayenne in a bowl and mix well. Chill, tightly covered, until serving time. Serve with grilled chicken or shrimp.

Yield: 2 cups

Southern Flavored Tea Syrup

6 cups water
20 tea bags
6 cups sugar
1/8 teaspoon baking soda

Combine the water and tea bags in a large saucepan. Bring to a slow boil. Remove and discard the tea bags. Add the sugar and baking soda and mix well. Pour into a 2-quart pitcher. Let stand, uncovered, until cool; the syrup will thicken as it stands. Store, covered, in the refrigerator for up to 2 weeks. To prepare tea, use 1 cup syrup with 2 quarts cold water. Recipe may be doubled.

Yield: 2 quarts

While faith makes all things possible, it is love that makes all things easy.

—Evan H. Hopkins

Margarita Garcia

1 (8-ounce) can frozen limeade
    concentrate
Ice
5 ounces tequila
3 ounces Triple Sec
1 lime, sliced
Coarse salt

Place the concentrate in a blender container. Fill with ice. Pour the tequila and Triple Sec over the ice. Blend until smooth and frozen. Run a lime slice around the outside edge of each glass; dip in salt. Pour the frozen mixture into the glasses. Garnish with lime slices.

Yield: 4 servings

John's Piña Coladas

4 ounces cream of coconut
4 ounces crushed pineapple
Ice
8 ounces spiced rum

Combine the cream of coconut and pineapple in a blender container. Fill with ice. Pour the rum over the ice. Blend until smooth and frozen.

Yield: 4 servings

Fruit and Mint Tea Punch

2 cups hot tea
3/4 cup sugar
1 cup orange juice
1/2 cup lemon juice
Orange, lemon and strawberry
    slices
Mint leaves
Ice cubes

Strain the tea over the sugar in a bowl. Add the orange juice and lemon juice and mix well. Let stand until cool. Add the fruit, mint leaves and ice cubes. Serve from a decorative jug or bowl.

Yield: 8 servings

CHRISTMAS PUNCH

2 cups sugar

2 cups boiling water

1 cup cold water

1 package strawberry Kool-Aid

1 (6-ounce) can frozen orange juice
   concentrate

1/2 cup lemon juice

1 (48-ounce) can pineapple juice

1/3 (1-liter) bottle ginger ale, or
   to taste

Dissolve the sugar in boiling water in a large stockpot. Add a mixture of the cold water and Kool-Aid and mix well. Add the orange juice concentrate, lemon juice and pineapple juice and mix well. Punch may be frozen at this point. Set aside some of the punch to prepare ice rings if desired. At serving time, add about 1/3 bottle of the ginger ale and mix well. Add crushed ice or an ice ring. To prepare the ice ring, mix fresh or frozen strawberries, sliced bananas, mandarin orange slices and /or pineapple tidbits with the reserved punch. Freeze in a ring mold.

Note: Christmas Punch is pictured on the cover.

Yield: 1 1/4 gallons

WASSAIL

1 gallon apple cider

1 cup cranberry juice

1 (56-ounce) can apricot nectar

1 (56-ounce) can pineapple juice

1/2 cup lemon juice

1 package cinnamon sticks

1 cup sugar

Rum or brandy (optional)

2 oranges

1 tablespoon whole cloves

Combine the apple cider, cranberry juice, apricot nectar, pineapple juice, lemon juice, cinnamon sticks, sugar and rum in a large saucepan. Simmer for several hours, stirring occasionally. Pour into a large punch bowl. Stud the oranges with the cloves. Place the oranges gently in the wassail.

Yield: 50 servings

Heart and Soul

Breads and Brunch

"All people smile in the same language." —Unknown

I Am the Child

I am the child.
All the world waits for my coming.
All the world waits with interest to see
what I shall become.
Civilization hangs in the balance
For what I am, the worlds of
tomorrow will be.
I have come into your world about
which I know nothing.
How I came, I know not.
I am curious.
I am interested.
I am the child.
You hold in your hand my destiny.
You determine largely whether I shall
succeed or fail.
Give me, I beg you, those things
which make for happiness.
Train me that I may be a blessing
to humanity.
—Author Unknown

Chocolate Banana Muffins

2¹/₂ cups flour
¹/₃ cup baking cocoa
1 teaspoon baking soda
³/₄ teaspoon salt
1³/₄ cups sugar
¹/₂ cup vegetable oil
3 eggs
1¹/₂ cups mashed bananas
1 cup miniature chocolate chips

Preheat the oven to 325 degrees. Grease 24 muffin cups, spray with nonstick cooking spray or line with paper liners. Mix the flour, cocoa, baking soda and salt in a medium bowl and set aside. Beat the sugar, oil and eggs in a large mixer bowl at medium speed until blended. Add the bananas and beat well. Add the flour mixture gradually, beating at low speed just until mixed. Stir in the chocolate chips. Fill each muffin cup ²/₃ full with batter. Bake for 20 minutes or until a wooden pick inserted near the center comes out clean.

Yield: 2 dozen

GINGER GEMS

1¼ cups sifted flour
¾ teaspoon baking soda
½ teaspoon salt
1 teaspoon cinnamon
½ teaspoon ginger
¼ teaspoon nutmeg
⅓ cup shortening
½ cup sugar
⅓ cup molasses
1 egg, beaten
½ cup boiling water

Preheat the oven to 350 degrees. Sift the flour, baking soda, salt, cinnamon, ginger and nutmeg together. Cream the shortening and sugar in a mixer bowl until light and fluffy. Add the molasses and egg and beat well. Stir in the flour mixture. Add the boiling water and mix well. Pour into nonstick muffin cups. Bake for 15 to 20 minutes or until the muffins test done.

Yield: 1½ to 2 dozen

GINGER MUFFINS

2¼ cups flour
1½ teaspoons baking soda
1½ teaspoons ground ginger
1½ teaspoons cinnamon
½ teaspoon freshly grated nutmeg
½ teaspoon ground cloves
1 cup unsalted butter
1 cup molasses
1 egg
1 cup sugar
Grated peel of 1 large orange
½ cup boiling water
⅛ teaspoon salt
¼ cup sour cream

Preheat the oven to 350 degrees. Butter 48 miniature muffin cups or spray with nonstick cooking spray. Sift the flour, baking soda, ginger, cinnamon, nutmeg and cloves together. Heat the butter and molasses in a small saucepan until the butter melts, stirring occasionally. Let cool. Beat the egg and sugar in a mixer bowl until light and fluffy. Add the flour mixture and molasses mixture alternately, beating well after each addition. Add the orange peel, boiling water, salt and sour cream and mix well. Fill the muffin cups ½ full. Bake for 15 minutes or until puffed. Remove to a wire rack to cool. May be prepared and baked ahead and frozen between layers of waxed paper in plastic containers. Thaw in the covered container.

Yield: 4 dozen

ORANGE MUFFINS

1 cup margarine, softened

1 cup sugar

2 eggs

1 teaspoon baking soda

1 cup buttermilk

2 cups flour

Grated peel of 2 oranges

1/2 cup golden raisins (optional)

1 cup packed light brown sugar

Juice of 2 oranges

Preheat the oven to 400 degrees. Spray miniature muffin cups with nonstick cooking spray. Cream the margarine and sugar in a mixer bowl until light and fluffy. Add the eggs and mix well. Dissolve the baking soda in the buttermilk. Add the flour and buttermilk mixture alternately to the creamed mixture, beating well after each addition. Add the orange peel and raisins and mix well. Fill the muffin cups 2/3 full with batter. Bake for 12 to 15 minutes or until the muffins test done. Mix the brown sugar and orange juice in a bowl. Spoon over the hot muffins while still in the muffin cups. May be frozen after baking.

Yield: 6 dozen

Many persons have the wrong idea about what constitutes true happiness. It is not attained through self-gratification, but through fidelity to a worthy purpose.

—Helen Keller

Yeast Muffins

1 envelope dry yeast
2 cups warm water
3/4 cup melted butter
1/4 cup sugar
1 egg
4 cups self-rising flour

Preheat the oven to 350 degrees. Dissolve the yeast in the warm water and set aside. Mix the butter, sugar and egg in a bowl. Stir in the yeast mixture. Add the flour gradually, mixing well after each addition. Fill greased muffin cups 2/3 full. Bake for 30 minutes. Batter may be stored in an airtight container in the refrigerator for up to 2 days before baking. *Note:* On the morning of a party, muffins can be baked for 15 minutes or until set. Let cool and store in an airtight container. At serving time, brush heavily with melted butter and brown for 10 to 15 minutes. To avoid any risk of salmonella, you may wish to use an equivalent amount of pasteurized egg substitute.

Yield: 2 dozen

Lemon Bread

Grated peel of 2 lemons
1 1/2 cups sugar
1 cup vegetable oil
6 eggs
1 2/3 cups flour
1/8 teaspoon salt
2 teaspoons baking powder
Lemon Icing

Preheat the oven to 300 degrees. Combine the lemon peel, sugar and oil in a large bowl and mix well. Beat in the eggs 1 at a time. Add the flour, salt and baking powder and mix well. Pour into 2 greased 5x9-inch loaf pans. Bake for 1 hour. Pierce the warm bread several times. Pour Lemon Icing over the warm loaves.

Yield: 20 to 24 servings

Lemon Icing

2 cups confectioners' sugar
Juice of 2 lemons

Mix the confectioners' sugar and lemon juice in a bowl. The icing will be thin.

Oatmeal Bread

1 envelope dry yeast
1/2 cup warm water
1 cup quick-cooking oats
1/2 cup whole wheat flour
1/2 cup packed brown sugar
1 tablespoon salt
2 tablespoons margarine, softened,
   or 2 tablespoons vegetable oil
2 cups boiling water
5 cups (about) all-purpose flour

Dissolve the yeast in the warm water. Combine the oats, whole wheat flour, brown sugar, salt and margarine in a bowl and mix well. Pour the boiling water over the oat mixture. Let stand until lukewarm. Add the yeast mixture. Stir in enough of the all-purpose flour to make a stiff dough. Turn onto a floured board. Knead for 5 to 10 minutes or until smooth and elastic. Place in a greased bowl, turning to grease the surface of the dough. Let rise, covered, until doubled in bulk. Punch the dough down. Let rise again. Preheat the oven to 350 degrees. Shape into 2 loaves and place in 2 greased loaf pans. Bake for 30 to 40 minutes or until the loaves test done. Let cool. Brush the tops of the loaves with margarine for a soft crust.

♥ *Note:* See page 184 for the nutritional profile of this recipe.

Yield: 24 servings

Friends are angels who lift us to our feet when our own wings have trouble remembering how to fly.

—Unknown

Sun-Dried Tomato Bread

1/2 cup dry-pack sun-dried tomatoes

1 envelope dry yeast or rapid-rise dry yeast

2 cups warm water

2 teaspoons salt

1 teaspoon dried basil

5 cups (about) flour

1 egg white

1 tablespoon water

Chopped rosemary to taste

Plump the tomatoes in hot water to cover; drain and cut into 1/4-inch pieces. Dissolve the yeast in 2 cups warm water in a large bowl. Add the salt and basil. Stir in enough flour to form a soft dough. Turn onto a floured board. Knead until the dough is smooth and elastic. Place in a greased bowl, turning to grease the surface of the dough. Let rise, covered, until doubled in bulk. Turn onto the floured board. Shape into an oblong loaf. Place on a baking sheet sprinkled with cornmeal or sprayed with nonstick cooking spray. Cover with a clean cloth. Let rise until almost doubled in bulk.

Preheat the oven to 400 degrees. Brush the loaf with a mixture of the egg white and 1 tablespoon water. Sprinkle with rosemary. Make a lengthwise slash in the top of the loaf. Bake for 25 minutes or until the loaf is brown and sounds hollow when tapped on the bottom.

Yield: 6 to 8 servings

Broccoli Bread

1 (10-ounce) package frozen
    chopped broccoli, thawed
1 large onion, chopped
4 eggs, beaten
1/2 cup melted butter
3/4 teaspoon salt
1 (6-ounce) package corn
    bread mix

Preheat the oven to 400 degrees. Mix the broccoli, onion, eggs, butter and salt in a bowl. Add the corn bread mix and mix well. Spoon into a greased 8x8-inch or 9x13-inch baking pan. Bake for 30 to 35 minutes or until the corn bread tests done.

Yield: 4 to 6 servings

Spinach Corn Bread

1 (12-ounce) package frozen
    spinach
4 eggs, beaten
1 cup cottage cheese
6 tablespoons melted margarine
1 medium onion, chopped
1/2 teaspoon salt
1 (6-ounce) package corn
    bread mix

Preheat the oven to 400 degrees. Prepare the spinach using the package directions; drain. Mix the spinach, eggs, cottage cheese, margarine, onion, salt and corn bread mix in a bowl. Spoon into a greased 9x12-inch baking pan. Bake for 30 minutes. Cut into squares and serve warm.

Yield: 8 to 10 servings

I have learned to use the word impossible with the greatest caution.

—Wernher von Braun

Pecan French Toast

4 eggs
2/3 cup orange juice
1/3 cup milk
1/4 cup sugar
1/4 teaspoon nutmeg or cinnamon
1/2 teaspoon vanilla extract
1 (8-ounce) loaf French bread,
    cut into 1-inch slices
1/2 cup chopped pecans

Whisk the eggs, orange juice, milk, sugar, nutmeg and vanilla extract in a bowl. Place the bread in a single layer in a buttered casserole with a tight-fitting cover. Pour the milk mixture over the bread. Chill, covered, overnight. Preheat the oven to 400 degrees. Sprinkle the pecans over the bread. Bake for 20 to 25 minutes or until heated through. Serve with maple syrup and melted butter.

Yield: 6 to 8 servings

Vidalia Onion Pie

3/4 cup crushed Cheese Nip crackers
1/4 cup melted butter
3 1/2 cups sliced Vidalia onions
1/2 cup butter
3 eggs
1 cup scalded milk
1 pound Cheddar cheese, shredded
1 teaspoon salt
1/8 teaspoon pepper

Preheat the oven to 325 degrees. Mix the cracker crumbs and 1/4 cup butter in a bowl. Press over the bottom and up the side of a pie plate. Sauté the onions in 1/2 cup butter in a skillet until tender and light brown. Beat the eggs lightly in a bowl. Add the onions, milk, cheese, salt and pepper and mix well. Pour into the pie crust. Bake for 40 minutes.

Yield: 8 servings

Egg Casserole

12 eggs
1/2 cup flour
1 teaspoon baking powder
1/2 green bell pepper, chopped
1/2 onion, grated
8 ounces mushrooms, sliced
2 tablespoons chopped parsley
1/2 cup melted margarine
1 pound American cheese, shredded
1 pound cottage cheese

Preheat the oven to 350 degrees. Beat the eggs in a bowl. Add the flour, baking powder, bell pepper, onion, mushrooms, parsley and margarine and mix well. Add the American cheese and cottage cheese and mix well. Spoon into a greased 9x13-inch casserole. Bake for 40 to 45 minutes or until the mixture is heated through and the vegetables are tender.

Yield: 10 to 12 servings

Brunch Cheese Bake

2 packages refrigerator crescent
    rolls
4 ounces sharp Cheddar cheese,
    shredded
4 ounces Muenster cheese, shredded
4 ounces Monterey Jack cheese,
    shredded
1/3 pound Swiss cheese, shredded
8 ounces cream cheese, softened
2 eggs, beaten
1/2 cup melted margarine
Poppy seeds

Preheat the oven to 350 degrees. Unroll 1 package of roll dough. Place in the bottom of a 9x13-inch baking pan sprayed with nonstick baking spray, pressing the perforations to seal. Mix the Cheddar cheese, Muenster cheese, Monterey Jack cheese, Swiss cheese, cream cheese and eggs in a bowl. Spread over the rolls in the pan. Unroll the remaining roll dough. Place over the cheese mixture, pressing the perforations to seal. Pour the margarine over the top. Sprinkle generously with poppy seeds. Bake for 30 minutes or until the bread is brown. Cool somewhat before cutting into slices.

Yield: 10 to 12 servings

Wonderful Cheese and Apples

---

4 ounces Camembert cheese with
   rind, cut into pieces
1 cup shredded Swiss cheese
4 ounces bleu cheese, crumbled
3 (8-ounce) packages cream cheese,
   softened
2 tablespoons milk
2 tablespoons sour cream
1¼ cups chopped pecans
Snipped fresh parsley to taste
6 to 8 apples, sliced
Lemon juice

Let the Camembert cheese, Swiss cheese and bleu cheese stand at room temperature for 30 minutes. Combine with 2 packages of the cream cheese in a large bowl and mix well; set aside. Line a 9-inch tart pan, quiche pan, pie plate or cake pan with foil, plastic wrap or cheesecloth. Stir the milk and sour cream into the remaining cream cheese in a medium bowl. Spread over the foil in the tart pan. Sprinkle with the pecans, pressing the pecans gently into the cream cheese mixture. Spread the Camembert cheese mixture over the top, pressing to the edges of the pan.

Cover tightly with plastic wrap. Store in the refrigerator for 2 to 3 days or longer before serving. Remove the plastic wrap and invert onto a plate. Peel off the foil. Sprinkle with the parsley. Surround with apple slices dipped in lemon juice.

Yield: 8 to 10 servings

Heart Strings

Soups and Salads

"Do not follow where the path may lead.
Go, instead, where there is no path and leave a trail." –Unknown

HEART GIFTS

There are no greater gifts in life
That we could thus impart,
Than gifts not of an earthly form,
But gifts found in the heart.
The gift of understanding
To one misunderstood;
The gift of love to melt a heart
That's made of stone and wood;
The gift of patience for a soul
With temperamental ways,
The great gift of forgiveness
For one who's gone astray;
The gift of reaching out a hand
To one who's lost his way,
To help them find the path again
And help them there to stay.
These are the gifts that others need
Much more than worldly things,
For when they're given, joy is felt
And hearts begin to sing.

—Sharon Lee Roberts

Asopao

1 medium onion, chopped

1 small green bell pepper, chopped

2 cloves of garlic, chopped

1/2 teaspoon oregano

2 to 3 bay leaves

1 tablespoon vegetable oil

2 ounces ham steak, cut into cubes

1 (8-ounce) can tomato sauce

6 stuffed Spanish olives

1/2 can chopped pimentos

1 pound shrimp and/or lobster

1 1/2 teaspoons salt, or to taste

4 cups hot water

1 cup rice

1 to 2 teaspoons Knorr seasoning
    with annatto, or
    1 to 2 pinches saffron

Sauté the onion, green pepper, garlic, oregano and bay leaves in the oil in a medium stockpot or Dutch oven over medium heat. Add the ham. Cook until the ham is brown. Add the tomato sauce, olives and pimentos. Add the shrimp and salt and mix well. Bring to a boil. Cook, covered, over low heat for 15 minutes. Add the hot water and mix well. Return to a boil over high heat. Add the rice and Knorr seasoning while still boiling and mix well. Cook, covered, over medium heat for 10 to 15 minutes or until hot. Cook, covered, over low heat until the mixture is thick and soupy and the rice is tender, stirring occasionally. Remove and discard the bay leaves. Ladle into soup bowls. Garnish with sliced red pimentos or canned asparagus. Serve with French bread and white wine.

Note: The annatto or saffron adds a yellowish color to the soup.

Yield: 8 servings

Andalusian Condiment Buffet Soup

2 tablespoons margarine

1 tablespoon olive oil

4 cups thinly sliced onions

3 tablespoons flour

1 (16-ounce) can tomato purée

4 (14-ounce) cans beef broth

1 clove of garlic, minced

1 tablespoon red wine

1 tablespoon Worcestershire sauce

1 tablespoon sugar

1$^1/_2$ teaspoons salt

$^1/_4$ teaspoon pepper

$^1/_4$ teaspoon oregano

$^1/_4$ teaspoon tarragon

$^1/_4$ teaspoon Tabasco sauce

$^1/_2$ teaspoon cumin

Melt the margarine in a 4- or 5-quart saucepan over low heat. Add the oil and onions. Cook until the onions are tender and slightly golden brown, stirring occasionally. Sprinkle the flour over the onions and mix well. Stir in the tomato purée and beef broth gradually. Add the garlic, wine, Worcestershire sauce, sugar, salt, pepper, oregano, tarragon, Tabasco sauce and cumin and mix well. Bring to a boil over high heat; reduce the heat to low. Simmer for 30 to 40 minutes or until the flavors have blended, stirring occasionally. Ladle the soup into bowls. Set out the meatballs, meats, vegetables, starches and garnishes on a buffet table and have guests help themselves.

Yield: 8 to 10 servings

Meatballs

8 ounces lean ground beef, browned, drained

1 tablespoon chopped green onions

$^1/_4$ teaspoon salt

$^1/_8$ teaspoon cumin

$^1/_8$ teaspoon oregano

$^1/_8$ teaspoon pepper

Preheat the oven to 500 degrees. Combine the ground beef, green onions, salt, cumin, oregano and pepper in a bowl and mix well. Shape into bite-size balls. Place in a shallow baking pan. Bake for 5 minutes.

Yield: 30 meatballs

Meats

(use any 2 or 3 of the listed meats)

10 ounces linguiça, chorizo or
  kielbasa, cut into ¼-inch pieces,
  fried until brown
¼ to ⅓ cup cooked tiny shrimp
12 ounces ham, cut into cubes,
  sautéed

Vegetables

1 cup chopped bell pepper
1 cup chopped cucumber
1 cup chopped tomato
1 cup chopped sweet onion
8 ounces fresh mushrooms,
  sliced, sautéed
8 ounces fresh carrots, sliced,
  cooked fork-tender

Starches

1 cup cooked sliced potatoes
1 cup cooked brown rice
1 cup croutons

Garnishes

3 to 4 hard-cooked eggs, coarsely
  chopped
1 to 1½ cups sour cream
4 ounces Cheddar cheese, shredded
2 to 3 limes, cut into wedges
1 (8-ounce) can garbanzo beans,
  drained
1 small can sliced black olives
½ cup chopped parsley

Grandma Brown's Chicken Chowder

1 (4-pound) chicken, cut up

1 quart water

1 teaspoon salt

1/4 teaspoon pepper

3 large potatoes, peeled,
    cut into cubes

6 medium carrots, peeled, sliced

3 medium onions, sliced

1 tablespoon salt

1/2 teaspoon pepper

1 (10-ounce) package frozen peas

1 2/3 cups evaporated milk

Combine the chicken, water, 1 teaspoon salt and 1/4 teaspoon pepper in a large saucepan. Cook, covered, for 1 1/2 hours or until the chicken is tender. Remove the chicken to a plate and let cool. Skim the surface of the broth. Add the potatoes, carrots, onions, 1 tablespoon salt and 1/2 teaspoon pepper to the broth and mix well. Cover and bring to a boil over high heat; reduce the heat. Simmer for 15 minutes or just until the vegetables are tender. Remove the bones and chop the chicken into small pieces. Add the chicken and peas to the chowder. Cook for 5 minutes. Stir in the evaporated milk. Cook until heated through.

Yield: 10 to 12 servings

Corn Salsa Chowder

1¹/₂ cups chopped onions

2 tablespoons margarine

1 tablespoon flour

1 tablespoon chili powder

1 teaspoon cumin

1 (16-ounce) package frozen sweet
    corn, thawed

2 cups salsa

1 (14-ounce) can chicken broth

1 (4-ounce) jar chopped pimentos,
    drained

8 ounces cream cheese, softened

1 cup milk

Cilantro (optional)

Sauté the onions in the margarine in a large saucepan or Dutch oven. Stir in the flour, chili powder and cumin. Add the corn, salsa, broth and pimentos. Bring to a boil; remove from the heat. Add ¹/₄ cup of the hot mixture to the cream cheese gradually, stirring until blended; add the cream cheese to the hot mixture. Add the milk and mix well. Cook until heated through; do not boil. Ladle into bowls or crocks. Top with cilantro.

Yield: 4 to 6 servings

The happiest people don't necessarily have the best of everything. They just make the best of everything.

—Unknown

Brown Stew

1 to 2 pounds chuck or stew meat,
    cut into 1¹/₂-inch cubes
2 tablespoons vegetable oil
4 cups boiling water
1 tablespoon lemon juice
1 teaspoon Worcestershire sauce
¹/₈ teaspoon minced garlic
2 onions, sliced
¹/₈ teaspoon allspice or cloves, or
    to taste
1 tablespoon salt
1 teaspoon sugar
¹/₂ teaspoon pepper
¹/₂ teaspoon paprika
1 to 2 bay leaves
6 carrots, sliced
4 potatoes, cut into cubes

Brown the beef in the oil in a large saucepan. Add the boiling water, lemon juice, Worcestershire sauce, garlic, onions, allspice, salt, sugar, pepper, paprika and bay leaves and mix well. Simmer, covered, for 2 hours. Remove and discard the bay leaves. Add the carrots and potatoes to the stew. Cook, covered, for 30 minutes.

Yield: 6 to 8 servings

Let your children know

often that you love them

just the way they are.

GAZPACHO

4 cups cold tomato juice
1 small onion, minced
2 cups freshly chopped tomatoes
1 cup minced green bell pepper
1 cucumber, chopped
2 scallions, chopped
1/4 cup freshly chopped parsley
1 teaspoon honey
1 clove of garlic, crushed
Juice of 1/2 lemon
Juice of 1 lime
2 tablespoons wine vinegar
1 teaspoon tarragon
1 teaspoon basil
1/8 teaspoon Tabasco sauce, or
    to taste
Salt and pepper to taste
2 tablespoons olive oil

Combine the tomato juice, onion, tomatoes, green pepper, cucumber, scallions, parsley, honey, garlic, lemon juice, lime juice, vinegar, tarragon, basil, Tabasco sauce, salt, pepper and oil in a large bowl and mix well. Chill for 2 hours or longer. May purée in a food processor if desired.

Yield: 6 servings

VICHYSSOISE

1 bunch leeks
1 large Vidalia onion, sliced
6 tablespoons butter
5 cans chicken broth
5 small red potatoes, peeled, sliced
1 tablespoon salt
1 teaspoon white pepper
Skim milk (optional)

Slice the leeks, using about 1/2 of the green stems. Sauté the leeks and onion in the butter in a large skillet. Add the chicken broth, potatoes, salt and white pepper and mix well. Cook over medium-low heat until the potatoes are tender; do not boil. Let cool. Process in a blender until well mixed. Chill thoroughly. The soup will be thick; thin with skim milk if desired. Garnish with chopped fresh chives.

Yield: 6 to 8 servings

GREEN CHILE STEW

2½ pounds lean ground round

1½ large onions, chopped

1 large clove of garlic, minced

5 (10-ounce) cans tomatoes with green chiles

6 (4-ounce) cans chopped green chiles

2 cups water

2 beef bouillon cubes

2 medium potatoes, cut into cubes

Salt to taste

Brown the ground round in a 5-quart stockpot, stirring until crumbly; drain well. Add the onions and garlic. Cook for 5 to 10 minutes or until tender. Add the tomatoes with green chiles, canned green chiles, water, bouillon cubes and potatoes and mix well. Simmer for 3 hours, stirring every 30 minutes. Season with salt. Serve with warm flour tortillas and butter.

Yield: 8 servings

Bonnie's Seafood Gumbo

1 large onion, chopped
6 cloves of garlic, minced
1/3 cup olive oil
1 bunch green onions, chopped
1 large green bell pepper, chopped
2 ribs celery, chopped
2 quarts tomatoes
1 (15-ounce) can tomato sauce
1 teaspoon cayenne
1 teaspoon black pepper
1 tablespoon Cajun seasoning
2 quarts water
2 1/2 pounds medium shrimp,
   peeled, deveined

Sauté the onion and garlic in the oil in a Dutch oven or 4-quart stockpot. Add the green onions, green pepper and celery. Cook until the garlic and celery are tender, stirring frequently. Stir in the tomatoes and tomato sauce. Stir in the seasonings. Add the water and mix well. Bring to a boil. Simmer for 1 hour. Add the shrimp. Cook for 3 to 4 minutes or until the shrimp turn pink. Adjust the seasonings. Serve over rice.

Yield: 20 servings

Write it on your heart

that every day is

the best day in the year.

—Ralph Waldo Emerson

CREAMY SHRIMP BISQUE

2 tablespoons margarine or butter

1 cup sliced fresh mushrooms

2 tablespoons sliced green onions

1 clove of garlic, minced

1 (10-ounce) can chicken broth

1 pound fresh medium shrimp,
    peeled, deveined

3 tablespoons flour

1/2 cup light cream

1/3 cup chablis

1 tablespoon chopped fresh parsley

Heat the margarine in a 10-inch skillet over medium heat. Add the mushrooms, green onions and garlic. Cook until tender, stirring occasionally. Add the chicken broth and shrimp and mix well. Bring to a boil. Blend the flour and cream in a cup. Stir a small amount of the hot broth into the flour mixture; stir the flour mixture into the broth mixture. Cook until the mixture returns to a boil and thickens, stirring frequently. Stir in the wine and parsley. Cook until heated through.

Yield: 4 servings

The strongest evidence of love is sacrifice.

Taco Soup

2 pounds ground round
1 onion, chopped
1 green bell pepper, chopped
1 envelope taco seasoning mix
1 envelope ranch salad dressing mix
1 (28-ounce) can crushed tomatoes
1 (10-ounce) can tomatoes with
   green chiles
2 cans Mexicorn
1 (16-ounce) can kidney beans
1 (16-ounce) can pinto beans
1 (15-ounce) can hominy, drained
Chili powder to taste
Shredded sharp cheese

Brown the ground round with the onion and green pepper in a nonstick skillet, stirring until the ground round is crumbly; drain well. Add the taco seasoning mix and salad dressing mix and mix well. Add the crushed tomatoes, tomatoes with green chiles, Mexicorn, kidney beans, pinto beans, hominy and chili powder and mix well. Simmer for 1 hour. Ladle into bowls. Top each serving with cheese. Serve with tortilla chips.

Yield: 4 to 6 servings

Grandmother Averitt's Banana Salad

2 eggs
³/4 cup sugar
Juice of 3 lemons
Grated peel of 1 lemon
¹/2 can salted peanuts, crushed
6 bananas, sliced into rounds

Beat the eggs in a bowl. Add the sugar, lemon juice and lemon peel and mix well. Pour into a double boiler. Cook for 5 minutes or until thickened, stirring constantly. Let cool. Reserve a small amount of the peanuts for topping. Mix the egg mixture with the bananas and remaining peanuts in a bowl, being careful not to mash the bananas. Serve in a crystal bowl. Sprinkle the reserved peanuts over the top.

Yield: 6 to 8 servings

Blueberry Salad

1 can blueberries
1 can crushed pineapple
1 large package raspberry gelatin
1 cup hot water
8 ounces cream cheese, softened
1 cup sour cream
¹/2 cup sugar
¹/2 cup chopped pecans

Drain the blueberries and pineapple, reserving the juice. Add enough water to the juice to measure 2 cups. Bring the juice mixture to a simmer in a saucepan. Dissolve the gelatin in the hot water. Add the gelatin and fruit to the juice mixture and mix well. Pour into a mold or dish. Chill overnight. Mix the cream cheese, sour cream and sugar in a bowl. Spread over the gelatin. Sprinkle with the pecans.

Yield: 4 to 6 servings

VACATION SALAD

1 (20-ounce) can crushed
  pineapple
1 cup sugar
Juice of 1 lemon
2 envelopes unflavored gelatin
1/3 cup cold water
2 cups shredded Cheddar cheese
1 cup whipping cream, whipped, or
  8 ounces whipped topping
Green Pepper Dressing

Combine the undrained pineapple, sugar and lemon juice in a saucepan. Cook until heated through, stirring until the sugar is dissolved. Soften the gelatin in the cold water. Add to the pineapple mixture, stirring until the gelatin is dissolved. Chill briefly. Add the cheese and whipped cream and stir gently until mixed. Spoon into individual molds or a 2-quart casserole. Chill overnight. Serve with Green Pepper Dressing.

Yield: 12 servings

Green Pepper Dressing

1 cup mayonnaise-type salad
  dressing
3 tablespoons minced green bell
  pepper
3 tablespoons minced onion
3 tablespoons minced celery
3 tablespoons sliced green olives

Combine the salad dressing, green pepper, onion, celery and olives in a bowl and mix well. Chill, covered, for 24 hours to allow the flavors to blend.

Ken's Caesar Salad

---

4 anchovy fillets, or
    2 (2-inch) strips of anchovy
    paste
1 clove of garlic, crushed
2 tablespoons Worcestershire sauce,
    or to taste
1/2 teaspoon dry hot mustard
1 teaspoon Dijon mustard
Juice of 1/2 lemon
2 tablespoons grated Parmesan
    cheese
1/2 cup extra-virgin olive oil
Romaine lettuce, torn into
    bite-size pieces
2 tablespoons grated Parmesan
    cheese
Croutons

Crush the anchovy fillets in a large wooden salad bowl. Add the garlic, Worcestershire sauce, hot mustard and Dijon mustard and mix until a smooth paste forms. Add the lemon juice and mix well. Add 2 tablespoons cheese. Add the olive oil gradually, beating constantly. Add the lettuce and toss. Top with 2 tablespoons cheese and croutons. Toss immediately before serving.

Yield: 4 to 6 servings

Black Bean and Corn Salad

2 cans black beans, drained, rinsed
1 (10-ounce) package frozen corn,
    thawed
1 green bell pepper, chopped
1 red bell pepper, chopped
3 green onions, thinly sliced
2 tablespoons minced fresh parsley
3 tablespoons salsa, or to taste
1/8 teaspoon salt
Freshly ground pepper to taste
2 tablespoons olive oil
3 tablespoons fresh lime juice
2 tablespoons red wine vinegar
    (optional)

Combine the beans, corn, bell peppers, green onions, parsley, salsa, salt and pepper in a large bowl. Add the oil, lime juice and vinegar and mix well. Serve over lettuce. May serve in a hollowed-out tomato or as a salsa over grilled fish or chicken.

Yield: 6 to 8 servings

Shades of Korea Cabbage Salad

1 package Oriental noodle
    soup mix
1 tablespoon sugar
1/2 cup vegetable oil
3 tablespoons vinegar
1/2 teaspoon salt
1/2 teaspoon pepper
1 medium cabbage, rinsed,
    chopped, spun dry
1 bunch green onions, chopped
1/2 cup sliced almonds
2 tablespoons sesame seeds
1/2 cup sunflower seeds

Break up the noodles from the soup mix. Combine the sugar, oil, vinegar, salt, pepper and seasoning packet from the soup mix in a bowl and mix well. Chill thoroughly. Mix the cabbage and green onions in a bowl. Chill thoroughly. At serving time, combine the cabbage mixture, crushed noodles, almonds, sesame seeds and sunflower seeds in a large bowl and mix well. Add the vinegar mixture and toss well. Leftovers may be stored in the refrigerator; the salad will wilt but still taste good.

Yield: 4 servings

My Green Jacket Salad

2 servings lettuce

1 tomato, peeled

Chopped parsley to taste

2 teaspoons (heaping) chopped
　green onions

1 teaspoon seasoned salt

3/4 teaspoon MSG

1/2 teaspoon oregano

1/2 cup vegetable oil

1/4 cup wine vinegar

Grated Parmesan cheese to taste

4 teaspoons (heaping) toasted pita
　bread croutons

Cut the lettuce into bite-size
pieces. Chill thoroughly. Mash
the tomato in a bowl. Add the
parsley, green onions, seasoned
salt, MSG, oregano, oil and
vinegar and mix well. Add the
lettuce and toss well. Divide
evenly among 2 salad plates.
Top with cheese and croutons.
Serve immediately.

Yield: 2 servings

Aunt Annie's Coleslaw

1 large (about 5 pounds) cabbage,
　shredded

2 medium onions, sliced

1 bell pepper, sliced

1 cucumber, sliced into halves or
　quarters

3/4 cup plus 2 tablespoons sugar

1 cup vinegar

3/4 cup vegetable oil

2 tablespoons sugar

1 teaspoon dry mustard

1 teaspoon celery seeds

1 teaspoon salt

Layer the cabbage, onions,
bell pepper and cucumber in a
bowl. Sprinkle 3/4 cup plus 2
tablespoons sugar over the top.
Combine the vinegar, oil, 2
tablespoons sugar, mustard,
celery seeds and salt in a
saucepan. Bring to a boil. Pour
over the cabbage mixture. Let
cool. Pack the cabbage mixture
into a jar; press down. Chill,
covered, overnight. Stir to mix
well and press down again. May
be prepared up to 1 week ahead
and stored in the refrigerator.

Yield: 6 to 8 servings

Molded Gazpacho Salad with Avocado Cream

2 envelopes unflavored gelatin

4¹/₂ cups tomato juice

¹/₄ cup wine vinegar

1 clove of garlic, crushed

2 teaspoons salt

¹/₄ teaspoon black pepper

¹/₈ teaspoon cayenne, or to taste

2 large tomatoes, peeled, chopped,
   drained

¹/₂ cup finely chopped green onions

³/₄ cup finely chopped green pepper

³/₄ cup finely chopped peeled
   cucumber, drained

¹/₄ cup finely chopped pimento

Avocado Cream

Combine the gelatin with 1 cup of the tomato juice in a saucepan. Let stand for 5 minutes to soften. Bring to a simmer, stirring until the gelatin is dissolved. Remove from the heat. Add the remaining 3¹/₂ cups tomato juice, vinegar, garlic, salt, black pepper and cayenne and mix well. Chill until the mixture begins to set. Fold in the tomatoes, green onions, green pepper, cucumber and pimento. Pour into a greased 6-cup ring mold. Chill for 3 hours or until firm. Unmold onto a plate. Garnish with parsley. Place the Avocado Cream in the center of the ring.

Yield: 6 to 8 servings

Avocado Cream

¹/₃ cup mashed avocado

¹/₂ cup sour cream

¹/₂ teaspoon salt

¹/₈ teaspoon cayenne, or to taste

Combine the avocado, sour cream, salt and cayenne in a bowl and mix well.

Poolside Salad

1 pound assorted lettuces, torn into
    bite-size pieces
1 pound fresh spinach, torn into
    bite-size pieces
2 medium avocados, sliced
1 pint strawberries, cut into halves
1 cantaloupe, cut into balls
1 pint cherry tomatoes, cut into
    halves
2 cucumbers, sliced
8 ounces fresh mushrooms, sliced
Poppy Seed Dressing

Combine the lettuce, spinach, avocados, strawberries, cantaloupe, cherry tomatoes, cucumbers and mushrooms in a large salad bowl and mix well. Toss with Poppy Seed Dressing just before serving.

Yield: 20 servings

Poppy Seed Dressing

1 cup vegetable oil
1/2 cup tarragon vinegar
1/2 cup sugar
1 tablespoon poppy seeds
1 teaspoon dry mustard
1 teaspoon grated onion
3/4 teaspoon onion salt

Combine the oil, vinegar, sugar, poppy seeds, mustard, onion and onion salt in a jar with a lid. Cover and shake well. Chill until serving time. May be prepared ahead and stored in the refrigerator.

Accept the challenges, so that you may feel the exhilaration of victory.

—General George Patton

Spinach Ring

2 envelopes unflavored gelatin

1/2 cup cold water

2 packages frozen chopped spinach

2 to 3 beef or chicken bouillon cubes

4 hard-cooked eggs, chopped

1/4 cup Worcestershire sauce

1 teaspoon salt

1 cup mayonnaise

Sour Cream and Horseradish
    Sauce

Soften the gelatin in the cold water. Place the spinach in a saucepan; do not add water. Cook over low heat until thawed and heated through. Add the bouillon cubes, stirring until dissolved. Add the gelatin, stirring constantly until dissolved. Mix the eggs, Worcestershire sauce, salt and mayonnaise in a bowl. Add to the spinach mixture and mix well. Pour into a ring mold sprayed with nonstick cooking spray. Chill until set. Serve with Sour Cream and Horseradish Sauce. May be prepared several days ahead and stored in the refrigerator.

Yield: 12 servings

*Sour Cream and
Horseradish Sauce*

1 cup sour cream

1 tablespoon minced onion

1/4 cup horseradish

Combine the sour cream, onion and horseradish in a bowl and mix well.

Mango Spinach Salad

Fresh spinach, torn into bite-size
    pieces
1 large mango, peeled, cut into
    1/2-inch cubes
1 medium red onion, sliced into
    thin rings
Juice of 1 lemon
Raspberry vinegar
1 teaspoon Dijon mustard
1/2 teaspoon dried tarragon
1/2 teaspoon salt
Freshly ground pepper to taste
1/2 cup canola oil

Combine the spinach, mango
and onion in a salad bowl. Mix
the lemon juice with enough
vinegar to measure 1/3 cup in
a small bowl. Add the Dijon
mustard, tarragon, salt and
pepper and mix well. Whisk
in the oil gradually. Toss the
salad with enough of the
dressing to coat lightly.

Yield: 6 servings

Asian Chicken Salad

1 1/2 pounds boneless skinless
    chicken breasts
4 ounces snow peas
4 ounces carrots, julienned
4 ounces celery, julienned
4 ounces jicama, julienned
6 ounces rice vinegar
4 ounces low-sodium soy sauce
2 tablespoons sugar
3 tablespoons minced fresh ginger
1 teaspoon freshly ground pepper
2 tablespoons chopped fresh
    cilantro

Grill the chicken until cooked
through. Let cool and cut into
julienne strips. Parboil the snow
peas, carrots, celery and jicama;
drain well. Chill the vegetables
thoroughly. Mix the vinegar,
soy sauce, sugar, ginger and
pepper in a small bowl. Combine
the chicken, vegetables, soy
sauce mixture and cilantro in a
large bowl and mix well. Chill
until serving time. Serve cold.

♥ Note: See page 184 for the
nutritional profile of this recipe.

Yield: 10 servings

Hot Chicken Salad

3 cups chopped cooked chicken
1/2 cup mayonnaise
2 cups finely chopped celery
2 tablespoons grated onion
2 tablespoons lemon juice
1/2 cup chopped almonds
1/2 teaspoon salt
1 teaspoon tarragon
1 cup crushed potato chips
1/2 cup shredded Cheddar cheese

Preheat the oven to 450 degrees. Combine the chicken, mayonnaise, celery, onion, lemon juice, almonds, salt and tarragon in a bowl and mix well. Spoon into a 7x11-inch baking dish. Top with the potato chips and cheese. Bake for 10 minutes.

Yield: 8 to 10 servings

Shrimp Under the Palms

8 ounces fresh shrimp, cooked
1 (8-ounce) can bamboo shoots, drained
1 (8-ounce) can artichokes, drained, cut into quarters
1 (14-ounce) can hearts of palm, drained, cut into bite-size pieces
8 ounces fresh mushrooms, sliced
1 pint cherry tomatoes
Herbal Vinaigrette

Combine the shrimp, bamboo shoots, artichokes, hearts of palm, mushrooms and tomatoes in a large bowl. Add the Herbal Vinaigrette and toss well. Chill, covered, overnight. Serve over beds of lettuce on individual salad plates.

Yield: 8 to 10 servings

Herbal Vinaigrette

3 cloves of garlic, minced
1 tablespoon salt
1 teaspoon pepper
3 tablespoons sugar
3/4 cup chopped parsley
1 1/2 teaspoons thyme
2 cups vegetable oil
3/4 cup vinegar

Combine the garlic, salt, pepper, sugar, parsley, thyme, oil and vinegar in a bowl or jar with a lid and mix well.

Heart-Smart Crab Salad

4 cups shredded lettuce
2 green onions, finely chopped
1/2 cup chopped green bell pepper
1/2 cucumber, sliced
1/2 cup frozen tiny green peas
1/4 teaspoon garlic powder
2 cups flaked crab meat
Low-Fat Yogurt Dressing
1/4 cup shredded part-skim
    mozzarella cheese

Line a 9x9-inch dish with lettuce. Add the green onions, green pepper, cucumber and peas. Add the garlic powder and toss well. Top with the crab meat. Pour Low-Fat Yogurt Dressing over the crab meat. Top with the cheese. Garnish with tomato wedges. Chill until serving time. May substitute boiled shrimp for the crab meat or use a combination of crab meat and shrimp.

♥ *Note:* See page 184 for the nutritional profile of this recipe.

Yield: 4 servings

Low-Fat Yogurt Dressing

1 cup plain low-fat yogurt
2 tablespoons light mayonnaise
1/2 teaspoon dillweed
1/2 teaspoon pepper
1/2 teaspoon prepared horseradish

Combine the yogurt, mayonnaise, dillweed, pepper and horseradish in a bowl and mix well.

Heart of the Matter

Bi-Lo

Meat and Poultry

"The miracle is this . . . the more we share, the more we have." –Leonard Nimoy

Volunteers

Many will be shocked to find,
When the day of judgment nears,
That there's a special place in heaven
Set aside for volunteers.
Furnished with big recliners,
Satin couches and footstools,
Where there's no committee chairman,
No group leaders or carpools.
No eager team that needs a coach,
No bazaar and no bake sale,
There will be nothing to staple,
Not one thing to fold or mail.
Telephone lists will be outlawed,
But a finger snap will bring
Cool drinks and gourmet dinners,
And treats fit for a king.
You ask, "Who'll serve these privileged few
And work for all they're worth?"
Why, all those who reaped the benefits
And not once volunteered on Earth.

Swiss Steak

1 1/2 pounds beef top round steak
2 cups sliced onions
1 (4-ounce) jar whole mushrooms,
    drained
1 (10-ounce) can beef broth
1/4 teaspoon salt
1/4 teaspoon pepper
1/4 cup water
2 tablespoons cornstarch

Preheat the oven to 325 degrees. Place the steak in a large oven-proof skillet, Dutch oven or baking dish. Mix the onions, mushrooms, beef broth, salt and pepper in a bowl. Pour over the steak. Bake, covered, for 3 hours or until the beef is tender. Mix the water and cornstarch in a small bowl. Stir into the broth mixture. Bake for 15 minutes or until the gravy has thickened.

Yield: 6 servings

Rita's Sweet and Tangy Brisket

1 (6- to 8-pound) beef brisket
1 apple
1 onion
3 (14-ounce) cans sauerkraut,
    drained
1 (1-pound) package dark
    brown sugar
1 (14-ounce) can tomatoes

Preheat the oven to 350 degrees. Place the brisket in a baking pan. Cut the apple and onion into chunks over the brisket. Mix the sauerkraut, brown sugar and tomatoes in a bowl. Pour over the brisket. Bake, covered, with foil, for 3 to 4 hours or until the brisket is tender. Let cool. Marinate, covered, in the refrigerator for 3 days. To serve, slice and reheat.

Yield: 8 to 10 servings

TENDERLOIN WITH RED WINE MUSHROOM SAUCE

1 (6-pound) tenderloin
Vegetable oil
Red Wine Mushroom Sauce

Preheat the oven to 450 degrees. Brown the tenderloin in hot oil in a skillet. Place in a roasting pan. Roast for 10 minutes per pound for rare or 12 to 15 minutes per pound for medium. Let stand for 10 minutes before slicing. Serve with Red Wine Mushroom Sauce.

Yield: 6 servings

Red Wine Mushroom Sauce

2 tablespoons butter
2 shallots, finely chopped
1 clove of garlic, finely chopped
8 ounces mushrooms, thinly sliced
1 tablespoon tomato paste
1 teaspoon Bovril (meat glaze)
1/4 cup red wine
1/4 cup madeira
2 cups chicken stock
2 tablespoons chopped parsley
1 bay leaf
2 teaspoons red currant jelly

Melt the butter in a skillet. Add the shallots and garlic. Sauté until tender. Add the mushrooms. Sauté for several minutes. Add the tomato paste and Bovril and mix well. Cook for 1 minute. Add the red wine, madeira and chicken stock. Add the parsley, bay leaf and jelly and mix well. Cook, covered, over low heat for 30 minutes. Remove the bay leaf before serving. For a thicker sauce, add 2 tablespoons arrowroot dissolved in 1/4 cup liquid.

Beef Tenderloin with Walnut Horseradish Crumbs

1 tablespoon olive oil

2 shallots, thinly sliced

1 teaspoon minced garlic

1/2 teaspoon fennel seeds

1 cup coarse fresh bread crumbs

1 cup finely chopped walnuts

1/2 cup prepared horseradish, drained, patted dry

1 tablespoon chopped fresh mint, or 1/4 teaspoon dried

1/2 teaspoon crushed red pepper

3 pounds beef tenderloin, trimmed, tied

1 1/2 teaspoons salt

1/2 teaspoon freshly ground black pepper

1/3 cup crème fraîche or sour cream

Preheat the oven to 450 degrees. Heat the oil in a small saucepan over medium heat. Add the shallots. Cook until tender. Add the garlic and fennel seeds. Cook for 30 seconds, stirring constantly. Mix with the bread crumbs, walnuts, horseradish, mint and red pepper in a bowl. Rub the tenderloin with salt and pepper. Place on a rack in a foil-lined shallow roasting pan. Spread crème fraîche over the top and sides of the beef. Press the bread crumb mixture into the beef. Roast for 45 minutes or until a meat thermometer inserted in the center registers 130 degrees for medium-rare, covering loosely with foil if crumbs brown too quickly. Let stand for 10 minutes before slicing.

Yield: 8 to 10 servings

Service is coming to be one of the biggest words in the English language. Life's greatest pleasure and satisfaction is found in giving. And the greatest gift of all is that of one's self.

–James Cash Penney, 1956

Cream Tacos

2 pounds ground beef
1 large onion, chopped
1 can chili with beans
1 can ranch-style beans
1 can tomatoes with green chiles
2 pounds Velveeta cheese,
    cut into pieces
1 cup whipping cream
Nacho chips

Brown the ground beef in a skillet, stirring until crumbly; drain. Sauté the onion in a nonstick skillet. Combine the ground beef, onion, chili, beans, tomatoes with green chiles and cheese in a slow cooker and mix well. Cook until the cheese melts. Add the whipping cream and mix well. Serve over nacho chips with sour cream, guacamole, lettuce, tomatoes, shredded cheese, scallions and black olives.

Yield: 8 to 10 servings

Spicy Glazed Meatballs

1 pound ground beef
1/4 cup dry bread crumbs
1 small onion, finely chopped
1 teaspoon salt
1 egg, beaten
1 cup chili sauce
1 (10-ounce) jar grape jelly

Combine the ground beef, bread crumbs, onion, salt and egg in a bowl and mix well. Shape into 1-inch balls. Place in a large skillet. Cook until brown. Add the chili sauce and jelly and toss lightly. Simmer for 20 minutes. Serve warm in a chafing dish or electric skillet.

Yield: 16 to 24 meatballs

Beef Biryani

1 medium onion, chopped

2 teaspoons vegetable oil

1 teaspoon ground ginger

1 teaspoon minced garlic

2 green chiles, chopped

2 medium tomatoes, chopped

1 teaspoon coriander powder

1/4 teaspoon chili powder

1 teaspoon salt, or to taste

1 pound stew beef

1/4 cup chopped fresh coriander

1/4 teaspoon garam masala
   (see Note)

1 teaspoon vegetable oil

1 cinnamon stick

5 to 6 cloves

3 to 4 bay leaves

6 to 7 black peppercorns

1 teaspoon cumin seeds

1 cup rice, rinsed

2 cups water

Sauté the onion in 2 teaspoons oil in a large skillet until golden brown. Add the garlic, ginger and green chiles. Sauté for 5 minutes. Add the tomatoes, coriander powder, chili powder and salt. Sauté for several minutes. Add the beef. Simmer until tender, stirring occasionally. Add the chopped coriander and garam masala and mix well. Heat 1 teaspoon oil in a medium skillet. Add the cinnamon stick, cloves, bay leaves, peppercorns and cumin seeds. Cook over medium heat until the cumin seeds pop. Add the rice and water. Bring to a boil; reduce the heat. Cook for 8 minutes or until the water evaporates.

Remove and discard the bay leaves. Layer half the rice, the beef mixture and the remaining rice in a shallow serving dish. Garnish with bell pepper rings, onion rings and almonds. Serve hot. May substitute chicken or other leftover meat for the stew beef.

Note: Garam masala, a blend of roasted ground Indian spices, is available at Indian markets and large supermarkets.

Yield: 4 servings

Cajun-Fried Quail

Quail
1% buttermilk
Self-rising flour
Coarsely ground pepper
Cajun seasoning
Peanut oil

Cut the quail into quarters, discarding the backbones. Place in a shallow dish and cover with buttermilk. Chill, covered, for 6 to 8 hours. Combine the flour, pepper and Cajun seasoning in a shallow dish and mix well. For every 1 1/2 pounds flour, use 2 teaspoons pepper and 2 teaspoons Cajun seasoning. Heat peanut oil to 350 degrees in a deep fryer or skillet. Add the quail. Fry until golden brown.

Yield: variable

GRILLED VENISON WITH CABERNET MUSHROOM SAUCE

Worcestershire sauce
Dried mustard
Beer
Juniper berries
Red wine
1 venison tenderloin
Cabernet Mushroom Sauce

Mix Worcestershire sauce, mustard, beer and juniper berries with enough wine to cover the venison in a pan. Add the venison. Marinate in the refrigerator for 24 hours. Drain the venison, discarding the remaining marinade. Grill over hot coals for 1 1/2 to 2 hours or until cooked through. Serve with Cabernet Mushroom Sauce.

Yield: 2 servings

Cabernet Mushroom Sauce

1 tablespoon butter
1 clove of garlic, minced
2 cups thinly sliced mushrooms
1/2 cup beef stock
2 teaspoons lemon garlic pepper
    seasoning
1/2 cup dry red wine
2 teaspoons cider vinegar
1 teaspoon Worcestershire sauce
1 teaspoon cornstarch
1 tablespoon beef stock

Heat the butter in a skillet until golden brown. Add the garlic. Sauté until tender. Add the mushrooms. Sauté for 4 minutes. Add 1/2 cup beef stock and lemon garlic pepper seasoning and mix well. Bring to a low boil. Add the wine, vinegar and Worcestershire sauce and mix well. Blend in a mixture of the cornstarch and 1 tablespoon beef stock. Boil until reduced by 1/2.

Blackberry and Port Venison

$^{1}/_{2}$ teaspoon crushed red pepper
$^{1}/_{2}$ teaspoon black pepper
1 teaspoon garlic powder
$1^{1}/_{2}$ tablespoons Creole seasoning
1 (2-pound) venison backstrap, cut
   into halves
1 cup flour
$^{1}/_{4}$ cup (about) vegetable oil
1 cup ruby port
1 cup blackberry jam

Mix the red pepper, black pepper, garlic powder and Creole seasoning together. Sprinkle half the mixture over the venison. Dredge the seasoned side with flour. Turn the venison over and repeat the process. Heat the oil in a Dutch oven. Add the venison. Cook for 4 minutes per side; do not overcook. Remove the venison to a serving dish. Drain the skillet and deglaze with the port for 2 minutes. Add the jam. Cook until thickened, stirring occasionally. Pour over venison.

Yield: 4 servings

Glorious Lamb Chops

$^{1}/_{2}$ cup low-sodium soy sauce
$^{1}/_{2}$ cup water
2 tablespoons lemon juice
2 tablespoons canola oil
1 tablespoon brown sugar
$^{1}/_{4}$ to $^{1}/_{2}$ teaspoon Tabasco sauce
1 teaspoon (heaping) minced garlic
$^{1}/_{2}$ teaspoon coarsely ground
   pepper
12 thick lamb loin chops, trimmed

Mix the soy sauce, water, lemon juice, oil, brown sugar, Tabasco sauce, garlic and pepper in a zip-top plastic bag. Add the lamb chops. Marinate in the refrigerator overnight, turning occasionally. Remove the lamb chops from the marinade, discarding the marinade. Grill the lamb chops over medium coals for 4 to 5 minutes per side or until cooked through. This marinade is also good with London broil or chicken breasts; amount may be halved or doubled.

Yield: 12 servings

Whatever you do, do with all your might. Whatever your work is, put everything you've got into it. Don't go at anything haphazardly, don't scratch the surface, don't give a job part-time attention; give it your best.

—Clinton Davidson

Rosemary Dijon Lamb

2 cloves (or more) of garlic, minced

1/2 teaspoon salt

2 tablespoons Dijon mustard

1 tablespoon soy sauce

1 1/2 teaspoons minced fresh
    rosemary

2 tablespoons freshly squeezed
    lemon juice

1/4 cup olive oil

1 leg of lamb, bone in or butterflied

Mash the garlic with the salt in a bowl. Whisk in the Dijon mustard, soy sauce, rosemary, lemon juice and oil. Pour half the mixture over the lamb in a shallow dish or pan. Marinate, covered, in the refrigerator for 3 hours to overnight. Preheat the oven to Broil. Drain the lamb, discarding the marinade in the dish. For a whole leg of lamb, place the lamb on a rack in a roasting pan. Broil until brown. Reduce the oven temperature to 325 degrees. Roast to desired degree of doneness. For butterflied lamb, place the lamb on a rack in a broiler pan. Broil for 10 minutes per side or until brown, basting every 10 minutes with the remaining marinade. Remove from the oven. Let stand for 10 minutes before carving.

Yield: 4 to 6 servings

GRILLED MARINATED PORK WITH SWEET MUSTARD SAUCE

1 pound lean pork tenderloins

3 tablespoons frozen orange juice
  concentrate

2 tablespoons grainy Dijon
  mustard

2 tablespoons vegetable oil

2 tablespoons honey

1 1/2 tablespoons reduced-sodium
  soy sauce

1 teaspoon minced garlic

1 teaspoon finely grated fresh ginger

Freshly ground pepper to taste

Sweet Mustard Sauce

Place the tenderloins in a zip-top plastic bag. Mix the orange juice concentrate, Dijon mustard, oil, honey, soy sauce, garlic, ginger and pepper in a bowl. Pour over the tenderloins and toss to coat. Marinate in the refrigerator for 5 hours to overnight, turning at least once. Remove the meat from the marinade, reserving the marinade. Let stand for 20 to 30 minutes or until of room temperature. Grill over medium heat for 18 minutes or until cooked through, turning frequently and basting with the reserved marinade. Serve with warm Sweet Mustard Sauce.

♥ *Note:* See page 184 for nutritional profile of this recipe.

Yield: 4 servings

Sweet Mustard Sauce

3 tablespoons frozen orange juice
  concentrate, thawed

2 tablespoons apricot or peach
  marmalade

2 tablespoons grainy Dijon
  mustard

1 tablespoon lemon juice

1 teaspoon grated lemon peel

1 teaspoon dry mustard

Combine the orange juice concentrate, marmalade, Dijon mustard, lemon juice, lemon peel and dry mustard in a small saucepan. Bring to a boil. Cook until heated through, whisking constantly until smooth.

Marinated Pork Tenderloin with Plum Sauce

1/4 cup soy sauce

3 tablespoons dry sherry

1 tablespoon brown sugar

1 tablespoon honey

1 teaspoon salt

1 green onion, chopped

1 tablespoon finely chopped
gingerroot or ground ginger

1 to 2 cloves of garlic, crushed

1 pork tenderloin

Plum Sauce

Combine the soy sauce, sherry, brown sugar, honey, salt, green onion, gingerroot and garlic in a bowl and mix well. Pour over the tenderloin in a shallow pan. Marinate in the refrigerator for 4 hours to overnight. Drain the tenderloin, discarding the remaining marinade. Grill or broil the tenderloin until cooked through. Serve with Plum Sauce.

Yield: 4 to 6 servings

Plum Sauce

1 medium onion, finely chopped

2 tablespoons margarine

1 (10-ounce) jar plum jam or
preserves

1/4 cup tomato-based chili sauce

2 tablespoons soy sauce

1 teaspoon ground ginger

2 teaspoons lemon juice

Cook the onion slightly in the margarine in a saucepan. Add the jam, chili sauce, soy sauce, ginger and lemon juice and mix well. Cook over medium heat for 5 to 8 minutes or until thickened, stirring constantly.

Roast Pork Marinated in Herbs and Spices

1 (1-pound) pork tenderloin
1 teaspoon salt
¹/₈ teaspoon pepper
¹/₄ teaspoon thyme
¹/₈ teaspoon ground bay leaves
1 to 1¹/₂ cloves of garlic, crushed
¹/₈ teaspoon allspice, or to taste
Olive oil

Trim any excess fat from the tenderloin; score the remaining fat to allow the marinade to penetrate. Mix the salt, pepper, thyme, bay leaves, garlic and allspice together. Rub into the surface of the tenderloin. Place in a bowl. Marinate, covered, in the refrigerator for 12 to 24 hours. Scrape off the marinade and dry the tenderloin with paper towels. Brown the tenderloin in a small amount of oil in a skillet. Preheat the oven to 325 degrees. Remove the tenderloin to a casserole. Bake, covered, for 30 to 45 minutes or until cooked through; do not baste or turn the tenderloin while baking. May prepare gravy from the cooking liquid. Marinade ingredient amounts are given for a 1-pound tenderloin; the amounts can be increased proportionately for larger tenderloins.

Yield: 2 to 3 servings

Pork Tenderloin in Saté Sauce

1/4 cup honey

1/4 cup smooth peanut butter

2 tablespoons hoisin sauce

2 tablespoons lime juice

1 tablespoon frozen orange juice
    concentrate, thawed

1 tablespoon finely chopped fresh
    gingerroot

2 cloves of garlic, finely chopped

2 tablespoons soy sauce

1/4 teaspoon Tabasco sauce

1 teaspoon sesame oil

1/3 cup finely chopped fresh parsley

1 (3-pound) pork tenderloin,
    trimmed

1/2 cup chicken broth

1/2 cup orange juice

Combine the honey, peanut butter, hoisin sauce, lime juice, orange juice concentrate, gingerroot, garlic, soy sauce, Tabasco sauce, oil and parsley in a bowl and mix well. Pour into a zip-top plastic bag. Add the tenderloin. Marinate in the refrigerator for 3 to 24 hours. Remove the tenderloin from the marinade, reserving the marinade. Place the tenderloin in a baking pan. Preheat the oven to 350 degrees. Bake for 45 to 60 minutes or until cooked through. Remove from the oven and cover with foil. Combine the reserved marinade, chicken broth and orange juice in a small saucepan. Bring to a boil. Simmer for 5 minutes, stirring occasionally. Serve the sauce with the tenderloin.

Yield: 6 to 8 servings

Chalupas

1 pound pinto beans, sorted, rinsed

2 to 3 cloves of garlic, minced

2 tablespoons chili powder

1 tablespoon cumin

1 teaspoon oregano

2 (4-ounce) cans chopped green
    chiles

Salt to taste

1 (3-pound) pork roast

Combine the beans, garlic, chili powder, cumin, oregano, green chiles, salt, pork roast and water to cover in a large Dutch oven. Simmer for 6 hours or until the roast is cooked through, adding additional water if needed. Shred the pork roast, discarding fat and bones. Return to the Dutch oven. Simmer for 1 hour or until the cooking liquid is somewhat reduced and thickened. Serve with tortilla chips, sour cream, guacamole, diced onions and peppers, shredded cheese, black olives and shredded lettuce.

Yield: 8 servings

Memphis Dry Rub Ribs

1/4 cup chili powder

2 tablespoons garlic salt

2 tablespoons onion powder

2 tablespoons sweet Hungarian
   paprika

2 tablespoons freshly ground black
   pepper

2 teaspoons cayenne

6 pounds spareribs

Honey Bourbon Barbecue Sauce

Soak some hickory chips in cold water for 30 minutes; drain and set aside. Combine the chili powder, garlic salt, onion powder, paprika, black pepper and cayenne in a small bowl and mix well. Rub on both sides of the spareribs. Let stand, wrapped in foil, for 1 hour. Place the wrapped ribs on the grill. Grill for 1 hour or until almost tender, turning frequently. Remove the ribs from the grill; cover loosely and set aside. Sprinkle the coals with the hickory chips. Return the ribs to the grill. Brush both sides with Honey Bourbon Barbecue Sauce. Grill for 10 minutes or until the sauce is glazed but not burned. Turn the ribs and brush generously with sauce. Grill for 10 minutes longer. Cut the ribs between the bones and serve immediately.

Yield: 6 to 8 servings

Honey Bourbon Barbecue Sauce

1/4 cup unsalted butter

1 large onion, finely chopped

2 cloves of garlic, minced

1 cup catsup

1 cup chili sauce

1/2 cup honey

1/2 cup lemon juice

1/3 cup bourbon or apple juice

2 tablespoons brown mustard

2 tablespoons Worcestershire sauce

1/4 teaspoon cayenne

Heat the butter in a saucepan over medium heat. Add the onion and garlic. Cook for 5 minutes, stirring frequently. Stir in the catsup, chili sauce, honey, lemon juice, bourbon, mustard, Worcestershire sauce and cayenne. Bring to a simmer; reduce the heat. Cook for 1 hour or until thickened, stirring frequently to avoid scorching.

Chicken Joseph

6 large chicken breasts, boned,
    skinned
2 tablespoons Dijon mustard
10 ounces cream cheese, softened
5 ounces bleu cheese, crumbled
1/2 cup butter, softened
1/8 teaspoon nutmeg, or to taste
1 cup shredded Swiss cheese
1 cup flour
1 egg, beaten
1 cup bread crumbs
Vegetable oil

Butterfly the chicken and open flat. Spread each piece with 1 teaspoon Dijon mustard. Mix the cream cheese, bleu cheese, butter and nutmeg in a bowl. Shape the cheese mixture into 6 small "eggs." Roll each "egg" in Swiss cheese. Place 1 "egg" on each chicken piece. Roll the chicken into an egg shape around the cheese mixture. Roll each piece in flour; dip in the egg, then in the bread crumbs. Secure with wooden picks if needed. Deep-fry the chicken in hot oil for 10 minutes or until cooked through. May instead brown the chicken in a sauté pan in melted butter and then bake at 400 degrees for 15 to 20 minutes or until cooked through.

Yield: 6 servings

Listen to a child and he will teach you something about love, faith and wonder.

Chicken Kiev

---

6 boneless skinless chicken breasts
Salt and white pepper to taste
1 cup unsalted butter
1/2 cup flour
1/4 cup milk
1 egg
1/2 teaspoon salt
Vegetable oil
8 ounces mushrooms, sliced
1 tablespoon minced shallots
1 cup light cream
2 tablespoons bread crumbs

Place the chicken between sheets of waxed paper. Pound as thin as Italian-style veal cutlets, being careful not to tear the chicken. Sprinkle with salt and pepper to taste. Cut the butter into pieces 1 1/2 inches long and 1/2 inch thick. Place 1 piece of butter on each chicken piece. There should be about 2 tablespoons butter remaining; set aside. Roll the chicken up from the long side around the butter, folding in the ends so that the butter is well enclosed. Chill, wrapped in foil, for 1 hour. Beat the flour, milk, egg and 1/2 teaspoon salt in a bowl until smooth. Heat 1/2 inch oil to 370 degrees in an electric skillet. Preheat the oven to 425 degrees. Coat the chicken thoroughly in the flour mixture. Fry in the hot oil until medium brown, turning as needed. Remove to a shallow baking pan. Bake for 5 to 8 minutes or until brown. Sauté the mushrooms and shallots in the reserved butter in a skillet until tender. Add the cream, bread crumbs, salt and pepper to taste and mix well. Bring to a boil. Pour the sauce on a serving platter. Place the chicken over the sauce.

Yield: 6 servings

CHICKEN BROCHETTES WITH RED BELL PEPPER AND FETA CHEESE

1 cup plain nonfat yogurt

5 tablespoons packed crumbled
   feta cheese

2 teaspoons minced garlic

1 teaspoon chopped fresh rosemary
   or oregano

1/4 teaspoon pepper

1 1/2 pounds boneless skinless
   chicken breasts, cut into
     1 1/2-inch pieces

2 large red bell peppers, cut into
     1 1/2-inch pieces

Salt and pepper to taste

Soak six 10- to 12-inch wooden skewers in water for 30 minutes; drain. Mix the yogurt, 3 tablespoons of the cheese, garlic, rosemary and pepper in a large bowl. Add the chicken, tossing to coat. Marinate at room temperature for 1 hour or in the refrigerator overnight for more intense flavor. Preheat the barbecue to medium-high or preheat the oven to Broil. Thread the chicken and red pepper pieces alternately onto the skewers. Season with salt and pepper. Grill or broil for 8 minutes or until the chicken is cooked through, turning occasionally. Place the brochettes on a platter. Sprinkle with the remaining 2 tablespoons cheese.

♥ *Note:* See page 184 for the nutritional profile of this recipe.

Yield: 6 servings

When we put our

problems into God's

hands, He puts His peace

into our hearts.

CRUNCHY SALSA CHICKEN

1 cup toasted wheat germ
1 teaspoon pumpkin pie spice
1 teaspoon ground cumin
1/4 teaspoon cayenne
2 egg whites
1 tablespoon water
4 boneless skinless chicken breasts
Orange Salsa

Preheat the oven to 400 degrees. Combine the wheat germ, pumpkin pie spice, cumin and cayenne in a shallow dish and mix well. Beat the egg whites and water in a shallow dish until frothy. Dip the chicken into the egg whites, then into the wheat germ mixture; repeat. Arrange the chicken on a baking sheet sprayed with nonstick cooking spray. Spray the top of the chicken lightly with nonstick cooking spray. Bake for 18 to 20 minutes or until the chicken is cooked through. Serve with Orange Salsa. May add 3/4 teaspoon salt to the wheat germ mixture.

♥ Note: See page 184 for the nutritional profile of this recipe.

Yield: 4 servings

Orange Salsa

3/4 cup chopped peeled orange
3/4 cup mild or medium
    chunky salsa

Combine the orange and salsa in a bowl and mix well. May add 1 tablespoon chopped cilantro.

Chicken Fajitas from the East

1 tablespoon hoisin sauce

1 tablespoon honey

1 tablespoon sesame oil

1 teaspoon chili paste

2 cloves of garlic, minced

1 tablespoon minced fresh
   gingerroot

8 boneless skinless chicken breasts

1 pound eggplant, cut into
   1/4-inch slices

2 large onions, sliced

8 (10-inch) flour tortillas

1/3 cup hoisin sauce

2 cups shredded lettuce

1/4 cup chopped fresh cilantro

Combine 1 tablespoon hoisin sauce, honey, oil, chili paste, garlic and gingerroot in a bowl and mix well. Combine half the mixture with the chicken in a zip-top plastic bag. Marinate in the refrigerator for 1 hour or longer. Brush the remaining mixture over the eggplant and onions. Preheat the grill or broiler. Grill the eggplant and onions until cooked through and brown on all sides. Remove the chicken from the marinade, discarding the marinade. Grill the chicken until cooked through and brown. Preheat the oven to 350 degrees. Cut the vegetables and chicken into 2-inch pieces and toss together. Wrap the tortillas in foil and heat in the oven for 5 to 10 minutes. Spread 1 spoonful of the remaining 1/3 cup hoisin sauce over the center of each tortilla. Divide the chicken and vegetables evenly among the tortillas and place in the center of each. Top with lettuce and cilantro. Fold up from the bottom to enclose the filling.

♥ *Note:* See page 184 for the nutritional profile of this recipe.

Yield: 8 servings

Stir-Fried Chicken with Raspberry Vinegar

1 pound boneless skinless
   chicken breasts
1/2 cup flour
2 teaspoons olive oil
1/2 teaspoon salt
1/4 teaspoon pepper
1 tablespoon chopped fresh
   rosemary
1/4 cup raspberry vinegar
1/4 cup dry white wine or
   chicken stock
2 teaspoons olive oil
8 ounces snow peas, trimmed
2 cups cherry tomatoes

Cut the chicken into 2-inch cubes. Pat dry and dust with the flour. Heat 2 teaspoons oil in a wok. Add the chicken. Stir-fry for 4 to 5 minutes or until cooked through, sprinkling with the salt, pepper and rosemary during cooking. Remove the chicken with a slotted spoon and keep warm. Add the vinegar and wine to the wok. Cook over medium-high heat until the sauce is slightly reduced, scraping the wok frequently. Return the chicken to the wok, stirring to coat with the sauce. Remove to a serving platter. Add 2 teaspoons oil to the wok. Add the snow peas. Stir-fry for 1 minute.

Add the tomatoes. Cook just until heated through. Spoon over the chicken. May substitute balsamic vinegar or other favorite vinegar for the raspberry vinegar. Serve with rice or couscous.

♥ *Note:* See page 184 for the nutritional profile of this recipe.

Yield: 6 servings

Kung Po Chicken with Cashews over Fried Rice

2 large chicken breasts

2 teaspoons cornstarch

¼ cup water or rice wine

¼ teaspoon salt

½ egg white

1 medium green bell pepper, cored, seeded

¼ cup vegetable oil

1 scallion, cut into short pieces

4 quarter-size slices gingerroot

4 to 5 small dried red chiles, soaked, seeded, shredded (optional)

2 tablespoons crushed yellow bean sauce

1 teaspoon Chinese rice wine or dry sherry

1 cup roasted cashews

Sesame oil

Fried rice

Cut the chicken into cubes about the size of bouillon cubes. Mix the cornstarch and water into a paste. Combine with the salt and egg white in a bowl and mix well. Add the chicken. Cut the green pepper into cubes or triangles about the size of the chicken pieces. Heat the vegetable oil in a preheated wok. Add the chicken. Stir-fry for 1 minute or until the color and texture of the chicken change. Remove with a slotted spoon and keep warm. Add the scallion, ginger, red chiles and green pepper to the wok. Stir-fry for 1 minute. Drain the chicken and add to the mixture in the wok. Add the bean sauce and wine and mix well. Stir-fry for 1 minute. Stir in the cashews and a few drops of sesame oil.

Serve hot over a bed of fried rice. Garnish with thinly sliced green onions. To reduce fat content in this recipe, other nuts such as peanuts, walnuts or almonds may be substituted for the cashews. An important feature of Szechuan cooking is that the texture of the nuts remain crunchy.

Yield: 4 servings

Barbara Bush's Barbecued Chicken

1 (3-pound) fryer, cut into quarters
1 large clove of garlic, crushed
1 teaspoon salt
1/2 teaspoon freshly ground pepper
1 tablespoon vegetable oil
3 tablespoons lemon juice
Homemade Barbecue Sauce

Combine the chicken, garlic, salt, pepper, oil and lemon juice in a heavy zip-top plastic bag. Shake to coat well. Marinate in the refrigerator for 24 hours, turning several times. Remove the chicken from the marinade, reserving the marinade. Place the chicken skin side up on the grill. Grill until very brown, basting occasionally with the marinade. Turn the chicken. About 20 minutes before the chicken is done, begin basting with Homemade Barbecue Sauce or your favorite bottled barbecue sauce. Grill until cooked through.

Yield: 4 servings

Homemade Barbecue Sauce

1/4 cup cider vinegar
2 1/4 cups water
3/4 cup sugar
1/2 cup butter or margarine
1/3 cup yellow mustard
2 onions, coarsely chopped
1/2 teaspoon salt
1/2 teaspoon black pepper
1/2 cup Worcestershire sauce
2 1/2 cups catsup
6 to 8 tablespoons lemon juice
Cayenne to taste

Combine the vinegar, water, sugar, butter, mustard, onions, salt and black pepper in a saucepan and mix well. Bring to a boil. Cook over low heat for 20 minutes or until the onions are tender, stirring occasionally. Add the Worcestershire sauce, catsup, lemon juice and cayenne and mix well. Simmer for 45 minutes, stirring occasionally. Adjust the seasonings. The sauce freezes well.

Chicken Curry

2 onions, finely chopped
2 tablespoons shortening
1 teaspoon minced garlic, or to taste
1 teaspoon ground ginger, or to taste
1 bay leaf
1 cinnamon stick, broken into pieces
1 cup canned tomatoes
1 teaspoon curry powder
1/2 teaspoon turmeric
Salt to taste
2 1/2 pounds chicken pieces, skinned
1 cup boiling water
1 tablespoon chopped parsley or
    cilantro

Brown the onions in the shortening in a skillet. Add the garlic, ginger, bay leaf and cinnamon. Sauté for 1 minute. Add the tomatoes, curry powder, turmeric and salt and mix well. Boil for 2 minutes. Add the chicken and boiling water and mix well. Cook, covered, over low heat until the chicken is cooked through. Sprinkle with the parsley. Serve with rice pullao.

Yield: 4 servings

Turkey Mexique

1 cup chopped onion
2 teaspoons minced garlic
1 teaspoon olive oil
1 to 2 tablespoons chili powder
1 tablespoon cumin seeds
1 tablespoon unbleached flour
1 1/2 cups chicken broth, strained
3 tablespoons tomato paste
3 cups chopped cooked turkey
1 green bell pepper, chopped
1/4 cup sliced pimento-stuffed
   green olives
1/2 cup water

Sauté the onion and garlic briefly in the oil in a large skillet. Add a splash of water. Cook until the vegetables are tender, stirring frequently. Stir in the chili powder, cumin seeds and flour. Add the chicken broth and tomato paste and mix well. Cook over low heat for 5 minutes. Stir in the turkey, green pepper and olives. Cook until heated through. If the sauce is too thick, add the water 2 tablespoons at a time until of desired consistency, stirring well after each addition. Serve over rice. May add 1/2 teaspoon salt when adding the chili powder.

♥ Note: See page 184 for the nutritional profile of this recipe.

Yield: 6 servings

Rosemary and Garlic Turkey

1 skinless turkey breast, bone in
2 cloves of garlic, cut into slivers
Small sprigs of fresh rosemary
3 tablespoons honey
1 tablespoon each Dijon mustard,
   olive oil and lemon juice
1/2 teaspoon pepper
Salt to taste

Preheat the oven to 350 degrees. Trim any fat from the turkey and cut slits in the top. Insert the garlic and rosemary into the slits. Mix the honey, Dijon mustard, oil, lemon juice and pepper in a bowl. Brush over the turkey. Sprinkle with salt. Place the turkey meaty side up in a roasting pan. Roast for 45 to 60 minutes or until cooked through, basting every 15 minutes with the pan drippings. Slice diagonally to serve. May be grilled instead of baked.

♥ Note: See page 184 for the nutritional profile of this recipe.

Yield: 8 servings

Great Venison Marinade

1 cup red wine
1/4 cup olive oil
1/4 cup soy sauce

Combine the wine, oil and soy sauce in a bowl and mix well. Pour into a dish and add venison. Cover and marinate in the refrigerator for 3 hours.

Yield: 1 1/2 cups

Old Charleston Barbecue Sauce

1/2 cup catsup
1/2 cup Worcestershire sauce
1/2 cup packed light brown sugar
1/2 cup white vinegar
1/2 cup water
2 tablespoons chili powder

Combine the catsup, Worcestershire sauce, brown sugar, vinegar, water and chili powder in a 2-quart saucepan and mix well. Boil until the mixture reaches the desired consistency, stirring occasionally. Serve with pork, beef or chicken.

Yield: 8 servings

Heart Warmers

Seafood and Pasta

"The grand essentials to happiness in this life are something to do, something to love and something to hope for." —Unknown

Precious Minutes

It only takes a minute,
To say, "I'm sorry, dear."
It only takes a minute
To wipe away a tear.
It only takes a minute
To walk the extra mile,
It only takes a minute
For a frown to be a smile.
It only takes a minute
To break a heart in two.
It only takes a minute
To say, "I'm sorry, too."
It only takes a minute
To decide life-changing things;
It only takes a minute
Even though we may be kings;
It only takes a minute
To decide for right or wrong,
It only takes a minute . . .
But it lasts a whole life long.

Sweet-and-Sour Fish Steaks

2 teaspoons olive oil

3 large onions, thinly sliced

2 cloves of garlic, finely chopped

1/8 teaspoon red pepper flakes, or
    to taste

1/4 cup raisins

2 teaspoons sugar

1/4 cup balsamic vinegar

1/4 cup dry white wine or water

Salt to taste

8 (4-ounce) pieces swordfish,
    halibut or tuna, 1 inch thick

2 tablespoons chopped fresh parsley

Preheat the oven to 425 degrees. Heat the oil in a large skillet. Add the onions, garlic, pepper flakes and raisins. Sprinkle with the sugar. Cook over medium heat until the onions begin to brown. Add the vinegar, wine and salt and mix well. Cook until the onions are tender and most of the cooking liquid has been absorbed. Adjust seasonings. Pat the fish dry. Arrange in a single layer in a baking dish. Top with the onion mixture. Bake for 10 to 12 minutes or until the fish flakes easily. Sprinkle with the parsley.

♥ *Note:* See page 184 for the nutritional profile of this recipe.

Yield: 8 servings

FISH IN CHIPS

1 tablespoon dry bread crumbs
1 pound perch or other fish fillets
1 cup crushed potato chips
1/2 cup grated Parmesan cheese
1/4 teaspoon dried thyme
1/4 cup milk
2 tablespoons melted butter or
    margarine

Preheat the oven to 500 degrees.
Sprinkle the bread crumbs in a
greased 8x8-inch baking dish.
Cut the fish into serving-size
pieces. Mix the potato chip
crumbs, cheese and thyme in a
shallow bowl. Dip the fish into
the milk, then into the cheese
mixture. Arrange in a single layer
in the baking dish. Drizzle with
the butter. Bake for 12 to 14
minutes or until the fish
flakes easily.

Yield: 4 servings

EDISTO SEAFOOD CASSEROLE

1 pound shrimp, peeled, deveined
1 tablespoon margarine
2 cups chopped Vidalia onions or
    other sweet onions
1 cup chopped celery
1/2 cup chopped green bell pepper
1/4 cup chopped red bell pepper
    (optional)
2 tablespoons margarine
1 (10-ounce) can cream of celery
    soup
8 ounces cream cheese, softened
1/2 cup milk
3 cups cooked rice
1 cup flaked crab meat
Salt and pepper to taste
Crushed butter crackers or
    stuffing mix

Preheat the oven to 350 degrees.
Sauté the shrimp in 1 tablespoon
margarine in a skillet; drain and
set aside. Sauté the onions, celery,
green pepper and red pepper in
2 tablespoons margarine in a
skillet. Add the soup, cream
cheese and milk and mix well.
Cook over low heat until heated
through, stirring frequently.
Add the rice, shrimp and crab
meat and mix well. Season with
salt and pepper. Spoon into a
buttered 11x14-inch casserole.
Bake for 20 minutes. Top with
cracker crumbs. Bake for
10 minutes.

Yield: 8 to 10 servings

CRAB ROLL-UPS

1 pound imitation crab meat, flaked
1/4 cup fat-free sour cream
1 cup fat-free ricotta cheese
1/4 cup grated Parmesan cheese
1 egg
1 tablespoon crushed dried parsley
1 teaspoon onion powder
6 lasagna noodles, cooked,
    rinsed in cold water
1 (15-ounce) can tomato sauce
Minced garlic to taste
Italian seasoning to taste
Pepper to taste

Preheat the oven to 375 degrees. Mix the imitation crab meat, sour cream, ricotta cheese, Parmesan cheese, egg, parsley and onion powder in a bowl. Spread on the noodles. Roll up the noodles and place seam side down in a 1 1/2-quart baking dish. Mix the tomato sauce, garlic, Italian seasoning and pepper in a bowl. Pour over the noodle rolls. Bake, covered, for 30 minutes.

Yield: 6 servings

GRILLED SALMON STEAKS WITH CANTALOUPE SALSA

2 teaspoons olive oil
1 tablespoon fresh lime juice
1 tablespoon soy sauce
2 (5- to 6-ounce) fresh salmon
    steaks
Salt and pepper to taste
Cantaloupe Salsa

Mix the olive oil, lime juice and soy sauce in a bowl. Brush over the salmon. Sprinkle with salt and pepper. Marinate at room temperature for 1 hour. Preheat the grill to medium-high. Drain the salmon, discarding the marinade. Grill the salmon for 4 minutes per side or until the center is opaque. Remove to serving plates. Spoon Cantaloupe Salsa alongside the salmon. Recipe may be doubled.

💜 *Note:* See page 184 for the nutritional profile of this recipe.

Yield: 2 servings

Cantaloupe Salsa

3/4 cup coarsely chopped
    cantaloupe
1/4 cup chopped red onion
2 tablespoons chopped fresh
    cilantro
2 teaspoons olive oil
1 tablespoon fresh lime juice
1 teaspoon minced seeded
    jalapeño
Salt and pepper to taste

Mix the cantaloupe, onion, cilantro, oil, lime juice and jalapeño in a small bowl. Season with salt and pepper. Let stand for 15 minutes.

Shrimp with Grits and Gravy

8 to 9 slices bacon

Grits

Shredded Cheddar cheese to taste
  (see Note)

1 pound medium or large shrimp,
  peeled, deveined

½ cup (or more) flour

1 medium Vidalia onion, chopped

½ to 1 small green bell pepper,
  chopped

4 to 5 cups milk

1 to 3 teaspoons instant coffee, or
  to taste

Salt and pepper to taste

Cook the bacon in a skillet until crisp; set aside. Drain the skillet, reserving the drippings. Prepare the grits using the package directions, omitting the salt. Add the cheese to the hot grits, stirring until melted. Cover and keep warm. Dust the shrimp lightly with some of the flour. Sauté in the skillet until the shrimp turn pink. Set the shrimp aside and keep warm. Return the reserved drippings to the skillet. Add the onion and green pepper. Sauté until tender. Add 3 tablespoons flour. Cook over medium-high heat until brown, stirring constantly. Stir in 4 cups of the milk gradually. Cook until thickened, stirring constantly.

If you want a thinner gravy, stir in some or all of the remaining milk or water. Crumble the bacon into the gravy, stirring constantly; reduce the heat. Sprinkle in the coffee powder, stirring until dissolved. Season with salt and pepper. Layer the grits, gravy and shrimp in individual bowls or plates. Serve with toast and fresh fruit.

Note: The gravy will be rich, so don't make the grits too cheesy.

Yield: 4 servings

Shrimp Creole

1 large onion, chopped

1 green bell pepper, chopped

4 ribs celery, chopped

2 cloves of garlic, minced

1/4 cup chopped parsley

3 tablespoons flour

1/2 teaspoon thyme

1 tablespoon chili powder

2 teaspoons Creole seasoning

1 cup water or chicken broth

1 teaspoon sugar

2 (14-ounce) cans tomatoes

1 tablespoon vinegar

1/2 (6-ounce) can tomato paste

1 pound shrimp, peeled, deveined

1 pound crab meat, flaked

Sauté the onion, bell pepper, celery, garlic and parsley in a nonstick Dutch oven until tender. Add the flour, thyme, chili powder, Creole seasoning, water and sugar and mix well. Cook for 5 minutes, stirring occasionally. Add the tomatoes, vinegar and tomato paste and mix well. Simmer for 10 minutes, stirring occasionally. Add the shrimp and crab meat. Simmer for 20 minutes, stirring occasionally. Serve with rice and hot sauce. May simmer for 30 minutes after adding the tomatoes, vinegar and tomato paste and then add precooked shrimp and crab meat; simmer for 10 minutes longer or until heated through.

Yield: 6 servings

Parchment Shrimp

*10 to 12 ounces medium shrimp,
    peeled, deveined*
3/4 cup chunky salsa
*1/2 cup shredded part-skim
    mozzarella cheese*
3 black olives, sliced

Preheat the oven to 400 degrees. Cut two 12x15-inch pieces from parchment paper or foil; fold in half lengthwise. Trim each piece into a large heart shape. Coat 1 side of each piece with nonstick cooking spray. Place on a baking sheet. Place half the shrimp on the coated side of each parchment piece. Top each with 1/4 cup of the salsa. Fold the hearts in half along the centers, pleating and crimping the edges together to seal. Bake for 10 to 12 minutes or until the parchment is puffed and lightly browned.

Cut an X in the top of the parchment and top each with cheese and olives. Bake for 1 minute or until the cheese melts. Serve with the remaining 1/4 cup salsa. May substitute Gruyère cheese for the mozzarella cheese.

♥ *Note:* See page 184 for the nutritional profile of this recipe.

Yield: 2 servings

Shrimp Etouffé

2 cups chopped onions

1 cup chopped celery

1/2 cup chopped green bell pepper

1 cup flour

1 cup vegetable oil

1 teaspoon Barbecue Seasoning

1 teaspoon basil

2 teaspoons seasoned salt

1/4 cup Worcestershire sauce

1/4 cup sherry

1 cup water

3 cups chopped tomatoes

4 ounces tomato sauce

16 to 20 tablespoons butter

8 to 10 tablespoons chopped
   green onions

40 to 50 ounces shrimp, peeled,
   deveined

1 1/2 quarts cooked rice

Combine the onions, celery and green pepper in a food processor container. Process until finely ground. For the sauce, cook the flour in the oil in a thick skillet over medium heat until the color resembles peanut butter, stirring constantly to prevent burning or sticking. Add the celery mixture. Cook for 10 minutes, stirring frequently. Add the Barbecue Seasoning, basil, seasoned salt, Worcestershire sauce, sherry and water and mix well. Cook for 1 minute, stirring constantly. Add the tomatoes and tomato sauce and mix well. Simmer for 10 minutes, stirring occasionally. Prepare the shrimp 1 serving at a time. For each serving, melt 2 tablespoons of the butter in a sauté pan. Cook until light brown. Add 1 tablespoon green onions and 1 cup of the sauce.

Cook until heated through, stirring occasionally. Add 5 ounces of the shrimp. Cook until very hot. Serve over rice.

Yield: 8 to 10 servings

Barbecue Seasoning

1/4 cup cayenne

2 teaspoons salt

2 teaspoons thyme

1/4 cup black pepper

2 teaspoons crushed red pepper

1/2 tablespoon oregano

Combine the cayenne, salt, thyme, black pepper, red pepper and oregano in a bowl and mix well.

Stuffed Shrimp with Hollandaise Sauce

24 jumbo shrimp
2 tablespoons butter
1 medium onion, finely chopped
1/2 red bell pepper, finely chopped
1/2 green bell pepper, finely chopped
1 clove of garlic, minced
1 tablespoon Cajun or Creole
    seasoning
1/2 cup fine dry bread crumbs
1 egg, lightly beaten
1/3 cup mayonnaise
8 ounces frozen crab meat, thawed,
    chopped
2 tablespoons butter
2 tablespoons lemon juice
2 tablespoons chablis or other dry
    white wine
Hollandaise Sauce

Preheat the oven to 400 degrees. Peel the shrimp, leaving the tails intact; devein if desired. Butterfly the shrimp by making a deep slit down the back of each from the large end to the tail, cutting to but not through the inside curve of the shrimp. Melt 2 tablespoons butter in a large saucepan. Add the onion, red pepper, green pepper and garlic. Cook over medium-high heat until tender, stirring frequently. Stir in the Cajun seasoning and bread crumbs. Mix the egg, mayonnaise and crab meat in a bowl. Stir into the onion mixture. Stuff each shrimp with about 3 tablespoons of the mixture. Arrange on a foil-lined 10x15-inch baking pan. Melt 2 tablespoons butter in a small saucepan. Stir in the lemon juice and chablis. Drizzle over the shrimp. Bake for 20 minutes. Serve with Hollandaise Sauce.

Yield: 6 to 8 servings

Hollandaise Sauce

1 cup egg substitute, or 2 eggs
1/2 teaspoon salt
1/4 cup lemon juice
1/2 cup butter, softened

Combine the egg substitute and salt in a large saucepan. Cook over medium heat until heated through, whisking constantly. Whisk in the lemon juice. Remove from the heat. Add 1/4 cup of the butter 2 tablespoons at a time, beating well after each addition. Pour into a blender container. Drop in the remaining butter 2 tablespoons at a time with the blender running at high speed. Blend until smooth. Return the sauce to the saucepan. Keep the sauce warm by placing the saucepan in a larger pan filled with hot water.

Shrimp Pilau

4 slices bacon

1 cup rice

1 teaspoon salt

3 tablespoons butter

1/2 cup finely chopped celery

2 tablespoons chopped green bell
    pepper

2 cups peeled shrimp

1 teaspoon Worcestershire sauce

1 tablespoon flour

Salt and pepper to taste

Cook the bacon in a skillet until crisp; drain, reserving the drippings. Add the reserved drippings and rice to salted water in a saucepan. Cook until tender; set aside and keep warm. Melt the butter in a large skillet. Add the celery and green pepper. Sauté until tender. Sprinkle the shrimp with the Worcestershire sauce; dredge in the flour. Add the shrimp to the vegetable mixture in the skillet. Simmer until the shrimp turn pink. Season with salt and pepper. Add the rice and mix well. Crumble in the bacon and mix well. Stir in additional butter if needed.

Yield: 6 servings

Tuna Steaks Glazed with Ginger, Lime and Soy Sauce

4 (1-inch-thick) tuna steaks
  (about 6 ounces each)
2 tablespoons fresh lime juice
1¹/₂ tablespoons low-sodium
  soy sauce
2 cloves of garlic, crushed
2 teaspoons grated peeled fresh
  ginger
1¹/₂ teaspoons sesame oil
1 teaspoon minced seeded jalapeño
  or other hot chile (optional)
¹/₂ teaspoon sugar

Arrange the tuna in a shallow ceramic or glass baking dish. Combine the lime juice, soy sauce, garlic, ginger, oil, jalapeño and sugar in a bowl and whisk until mixed. Pour over the tuna, turning to coat the tuna. Marinate, covered with plastic wrap, at room temperature for 30 minutes or in the refrigerator for 1 hour, turning once or twice and spooning the marinade over the fish. Preheat the oven to Broil. Place the fish in a broiler pan or ridged foil pan. Spoon the marinade over the fish. Broil 4 inches from the heat source for 3 minutes or until glazed and golden brown, basting twice with the marinade. Turn the fish and baste with the marinade.

Broil for 3 minutes or until glazed and cooked through, basting once with the marinade; do not overcook. Remove the fish to serving plates. Spoon the pan juices over the fish.

♥ *Note:* See page 184 for the nutritional profile of this recipe.

Yield: 4 servings

Lasagna

1 pound ground beef or turkey

1 clove of garlic, minced

1 tablespoon chopped fresh or
   dried parsley

1 tablespoon basil

1½ teaspoons salt

1 (16-ounce) can tomatoes

2 (6-ounce) cans tomato paste

24 ounces 4% milkfat cottage cheese

2 eggs, beaten

2 teaspoons salt

½ teaspoon pepper

2 tablespoons chopped fresh or
   dried parsley

½ cup grated Parmesan cheese

8 ounces lasagna, cooked, drained

1 pound mozzarella cheese, sliced
   or shredded

Brown the ground beef in a skillet, stirring until crumbly; drain well. Add the garlic, 1 tablespoon parsley, basil, 1½ teaspoons salt, tomatoes and tomato paste and mix well. Simmer for 45 minutes. Preheat the oven to 375 degrees. Drain any excess liquid from the cottage cheese. Combine the cottage cheese, eggs, 2 teaspoons salt, pepper, 2 tablespoons parsley and Parmesan cheese in a bowl and mix well. Layer the lasagna noodles, cottage cheese mixture, mozzarella cheese and ground beef mixture ½ at a time in a greased 9x13-inch glass baking dish or metal baking pan.

Bake for 30 minutes or until bubbly. Let stand for 10 minutes before cutting. May be prepared ahead without baking and refrigerated or frozen. Refrigerated lasagna may need to be baked for an extra 10 minutes; thaw frozen lasagna in the refrigerator overnight.

Yield: 8 servings

Chicken Spaghetti

1 hen
1 (16-ounce) package spaghetti
1 cup each chopped celery, onion
    and green bell pepper
1 (14- to 16-ounce) can tomatoes,
    finely chopped
2 tablespoons Worcestershire sauce
2 tablespoons lemon juice
1 (4-ounce) jar mushrooms, sliced
1 pound sharp Cheddar cheese,
    shredded

Preheat the oven to 350 degrees. Boil the chicken in water to cover in a saucepan until tender. Strain the broth and set aside. Chop the chicken, discarding the skin and bones. Cook the spaghetti in the chicken broth in a saucepan until most of the liquid is absorbed. Sauté the celery, onion and green pepper in a skillet sprayed with nonstick cooking spray. Add the remaining ingredients and mix well. Spoon into a 9x13-inch glass baking dish. Bake, covered with foil, for 30 minutes.

Yield: 10 to 12 servings

Mexican Spaghetti

1 large onion, chopped
2 cloves of garlic, minced
1 (14-ounce) can chicken broth
2 (14-ounce) cans chopped
    tomatoes
8 ounces spaghetti, broken into
    pieces
1½ cups mild to hot picante sauce
1 teaspoon ground cumin
2 cups chopped cooked chicken
    breast
1 cup shredded nonfat Cheddar
    cheese

Preheat the oven to 350 degrees. Combine the onion and garlic in a large skillet or saucepan sprayed with nonstick cooking spray. Sauté for 5 minutes. Add the chicken broth and undrained tomatoes. Add the spaghetti, picante sauce and cumin and mix well. Simmer, covered, until the spaghetti is al dente and most of the liquid is absorbed, stirring frequently. Add the chicken and mix well. Spoon into an 8x11-inch casserole sprayed with nonstick cooking spray. Sprinkle with the cheese. Bake, covered, for 15 to 20 minutes or until the cheese melts.

♥ Note: See page 184 for the nutritional profile of this recipe. If sodium is a concern, try using low-sodium or no-sodium chicken broth, tomatoes and picante sauce.

Yield: 6 servings

*S*EAFOOD *P*ASTA

1 onion, chopped
1/2 to 3/4 green bell pepper, chopped
1 cup sliced fresh mushrooms
1 hot pepper, chopped, or hot
    pepper sauce to taste
1 pound crab meat, chopped
1 (10-ounce) can Healthy Request
    mushroom soup
3/4 soup can water
Old Bay seasoning to taste
Garlic powder and onion powder
    to taste
Chopped basil to taste
Pepper to taste
1 cup scallops
1 cup shrimp
16 ounces fettuccini, linguini or
    other pasta, cooked, drained

Sauté the onion, green pepper, mushrooms and hot pepper in a large nonstick skillet or wok. Remove the vegetables or push to 1 side. Add the crab meat. Sauté briefly. Mix the vegetables back in. Add the soup and water and mix well. Add Old Bay seasoning, garlic powder, onion powder, basil and pepper and mix well. Simmer, covered, for 15 to 20 minutes or until heated through. Add the scallops and shrimp and mix well. Simmer for 5 minutes or until the shrimp turn pink. Serve over the pasta or mix with the pasta.

♥ *Note:* See page 184 for the nutritional profile of this recipe. If sodium is a concern, omitting the scallops will reduce the sodium by almost 1/2.

Yield: 6 servings

Shrimp Casseroles

4 cloves of garlic, minced
1/2 cup chopped onion
1 cup mushroom pieces
1 1/2 cups margarine
1/2 cup flour
1 teaspoon salt
1/2 teaspoon white pepper
1 teaspoon MSG
4 cups milk
8 ounces Velveeta cheese, shredded
4 ounces mozzarella cheese,
　shredded
8 ounces sharp Cheddar cheese,
　shredded
2 small cans grated Parmesan
　cheese

1 cup creamed cottage cheese
2 cups sour cream
7 cups shrimp, peeled, deveined,
　cooked
3 cups elbow macaroni, cooked
Buttered bread crumbs or
　cracker crumbs

Preheat the oven to 350 degrees. Sauté the garlic, onion and mushrooms in 1/2 cup of the margarine in a skillet until tender; set aside. Melt the remaining 1 cup margarine in a saucepan over low heat. Add the flour, salt, pepper and MSG and mix well. Cook until heated through, stirring constantly until smooth; do not brown. Remove from the heat. Add the milk gradually, stirring constantly. Cook over low heat just until bubbly, stirring constantly.

Combine the Velveeta cheese, mozzarella cheese, Cheddar cheese, Parmesan cheese, cottage cheese and sour cream in a large bowl. Add the shrimp, macaroni, onion mixture and cream sauce and mix well. Spoon into 2 lightly greased 3-quart casseroles. Top with bread crumbs. Bake for 30 minutes. May be frozen before topping with bread crumbs; thaw completely before baking.

Yield: 12 to 15 servings

Shrimp with Angel Hair Pasta

1/4 cup olive oil

6 scallions or spring onions, chopped

1 tablespoon chopped garlic

2 pounds small shrimp, peeled, deveined

12 black olives, pitted, cut into 1/4-inch slices

1 (1-quart) jar marinara sauce

1 (16-ounce) package angel hair pasta

2 teaspoons butter

Grated Parmesan cheese

Red pepper flakes to taste

Heat the oil in a 10-inch or larger skillet over medium heat for 2 minutes. Add the scallions and garlic. Sauté until translucent. Add the shrimp. Cook for 3 minutes or until the shrimp are slightly pink, stirring constantly. Add the olives and marinara sauce and mix well. Cook for 3 minutes or until the shrimp turn pink and the mixture is heated through, stirring constantly. Cook the pasta using the package directions; drain. Toss the pasta with the butter in a bowl. Top with the shrimp mixture. Serve the grated cheese and pepper flakes on the side.

Yield: 4 to 6 servings

I do not know what the future holds but I know who holds it in His hands.

Low-Country Fettuccini

1 head broccoli, broken into pieces,
    or 1 cup frozen tiny green peas
1/3 cup (about) butter
2 tablespoons chopped pimento
8 ounces small bay scallops
1 pound small shrimp, peeled,
    deveined
8 ounces crab meat
1 teaspoon salt
1/2 teaspoon pepper
Sherry or white wine to taste
Garlic Dill Cream Sauce
8 ounces fettuccini, cooked, drained

Steam the broccoli for several minutes in the microwave or prepare the peas using the package directions. Melt the butter in a skillet. Add the pimento, scallops, shrimp, crab meat, salt and pepper. Sauté for 2 to 3 minutes or until the shrimp turn slightly pink. Stir in the sherry. Cook for 1 minute or just until the shrimp turn pink. Stir in the Garlic Dill Cream Sauce and broccoli. Divide the pasta among individual serving plates. Ladle the shrimp mixture over the pasta. Garnish with fresh parsley. Serve immediately. May substitute angel hair pasta for the fettuccini.

Yield: 4 to 6 servings

Garlic Dill Cream Sauce

1/3 cup (about) butter
2 teaspoons self-rising flour
2 cups half-and-half
1 teaspoon sugar
1 teaspoon dried dillweed
1 teaspoon garlic powder

Melt the butter in a saucepan. Add the flour and blend well. Cook for 5 minutes, stirring constantly. Add the half-and-half gradually, stirring constantly. Add the sugar, dillweed and garlic powder. Cook until thickened, stirring constantly.

FETTUCCINI WITH FRESH TOMATO SAUCE

*16 to 24 ounces fettuccini or
  spaghetti*
Fresh Tomato Sauce
1/2 cup grated Parmesan cheese
8 ounces feta cheese, crumbled
*6 ounces mozzarella cheese, cut
  into cubes*

Cook the fettuccini using the
package directions; drain. Spoon
into a serving bowl. Ladle Fresh
Tomato Sauce over the top. Top
with Parmesan cheese, feta
cheese and mozzarella cheese.

Yield: 4 to 6 servings

Fresh Tomato Sauce

*6 large vine-ripened tomatoes,
  peeled*
1/4 cup extra-virgin olive oil
5 cloves of garlic, minced
1/2 cup sliced black olives
2 tablespoons chopped fresh basil
2 tablespoons chopped fresh parsley
1/2 teaspoon pepper
1/2 teaspoon salt

Chop the tomatoes coarsely
over a bowl, reserving the juice.
Combine the tomatoes, reserved
juice, oil, garlic, olives, basil,
parsley, pepper and salt in a large
bowl and mix well. Let stand,
covered, at room temperature
for 1 hour.

*Some people grin and
bear it. Others smile
and change it.*

Pasta and Vegetables with Peanut Sauce

3 tablespoons peanut butter

1 tablespoon hoisin sauce

2 tablespoons soy sauce

2 tablespoons lemon juice

1 tablespoon honey

2 teaspoons sesame oil

1 teaspoon hot chile paste or red
    pepper flakes

1/4 cup warm water

2 teaspoons vegetable oil

3 cloves of garlic, minced

1 tablespoon chopped fresh ginger

3 green onions, chopped

4 ounces fresh shiitake mushrooms
    or button mushrooms, sliced

1 red bell pepper, sliced

16 ounces spaghetti, cooked,
    drained

Florets of 1 bunch broccoli, cooked,
    drained

2 carrots, thinly sliced, cooked,
    drained

1/3 cup chopped fresh cilantro

1/3 cup chopped fresh basil

Combine the peanut butter, hoisin sauce, soy sauce, lemon juice, honey, sesame oil, chile paste and warm water in a bowl and mix well; set aside. Heat the vegetable oil in a wok or skillet. Add the garlic, ginger and green onions and mix gently. Cook for 1 to 2 minutes or until fragrant, stirring gently. Add the mushrooms and red pepper and mix well. Cook until the mushrooms and red pepper are tender. Add the peanut butter mixture and mix well. Cook for 1 minute or until heated through. Combine with the spaghetti, broccoli and carrots in a large bowl and mix well. Toss with the cilantro and basil.

♥ *Note:* See page 184 for the nutritional profile of this recipe.

Yield: 8 servings

MEDITERRANEAN ORZO

1 cup orzo
1 cup water
¹/₂ ounce sun-dried tomatoes
   (without oil)
1 ounce feta cheese, crumbled
¹/₄ cup chopped purple onion
¹/₄ cup chopped yellow bell pepper
¹/₄ cup chopped green bell pepper
¹/₄ cup chopped red bell pepper
2 tablespoons chopped fresh parsley
2 tablespoons sliced black olives
¹/₄ teaspoon pepper
2 tablespoons red wine vinegar
1¹/₂ teaspoons olive oil

Cook the orzo using the package directions, omitting any salt and fat; drain well. Bring 1 cup water to a boil in a small saucepan. Add the tomatoes. Cook for 2 minutes or until tender; drain. Chop the tomatoes. Combine the pasta, tomatoes, cheese, onion, bell peppers, parsley, olives, pepper, vinegar and oil in a large bowl and toss well. May omit the tomatoes and add salt to taste.

♥ *Note:* See page 184 for the nutritional profile of this recipe.

Yield: 4 servings

It takes vision and courage to create. It takes faith and courage to prove.

—Owen D. Young

Penne with Four Cheeses

---

4 quarts water

1 tablespoon salt

9 to 12 ounces penne

1 tablespoon butter

1/2 cup whipping cream

1/3 cup freshly grated Parmigiano-
   Reggiano cheese

4 ounces fontina cheese, shredded

2 ounces Gorgonzola cheese,
   crumbled

2 ounces mascarpone cheese

Salt and freshly ground pepper
   to taste

Preheat the oven to 450 degrees. Bring the water to a boil in a large saucepan or stockpot. Add 1 tablespoon salt. Drop in the pasta all at once, stirring well. Cook until almost al dente; drain. Heat the butter and whipping cream in a saucepan over low heat until the butter melts, stirring constantly. Reserve 2 tablespoons of the Parmigiano-Reggiano cheese. Add the remaining Parmigiano-Reggiano cheese, fontina cheese, Gorgonzola cheese and mascarpone cheese to the cream mixture. Cook until the cheeses have melted, stirring constantly.

Season with salt and pepper to taste. Remove from the heat. Combine the sauce and pasta in a large bowl, tossing well. Spoon into a casserole. Sprinkle with the reserved cheese. Bake for 10 to 15 minutes or until golden brown. Let stand for 5 minutes before serving.

Yield: 3 to 4 servings

Penne with Tomatoes, Olives and Two Cheeses

3 tablespoons olive oil

1 1/2 cups chopped onions

1 teaspoon minced garlic

3 (28-ounce) cans Italian plum
  tomatoes, drained

2 teaspoons dried basil

1 1/2 teaspoons crushed dried
  red pepper

2 cups canned low-sodium
  chicken broth

Salt and black pepper to taste

1 pound penne or rigatoni

3 tablespoons olive oil

2 1/2 cups packed shredded
  Havarti cheese

1/3 cup sliced pitted kalamata olives
  or other brine-cured olives

1/3 cup grated Parmesan cheese

1/4 cup finely chopped fresh basil

Heat 3 tablespoons oil in a large heavy Dutch oven over medium-high heat. Add the onions and garlic. Sauté for 5 minutes or until the onions are translucent. Stir in the tomatoes, dried basil and red pepper. Bring to a boil, breaking up the tomatoes with the back of a spoon. Add the chicken broth. Return to a boil; reduce the heat to medium. Simmer for 1 hour and 10 minutes or until the mixture is thickened and reduced to 6 cups, stirring occasionally. Season with salt and black pepper. Preheat the oven to 375 degrees. Cook the pasta in boiling salted water in a large stockpot until al dente; drain well. Return the pasta to the stockpot. Toss with 3 tablespoons oil. Pour the sauce over the pasta and mix well.

Stir in the Havarti cheese. Spoon into a 9x13-inch glass baking dish. Sprinkle with the olives and Parmesan cheese. Bake for 30 minutes or until heated through. Sprinkle with the fresh basil.

Yield: 4 servings

Lentil Spaghetti Sauce

1 medium onion, chopped
1 clove of garlic, minced
2 tablespoons vegetable oil
1 1/2 cups dried lentils, rinsed
1 dried hot red pepper, crumbled
4 cups low-sodium chicken broth
Fresh ground black pepper to taste
1/4 teaspoon dried basil
1/4 teaspoon dried oregano
2 tablespoons tomato paste
1 tablespoon vinegar
2 teaspoons sugar

Sauté the onion and garlic in the oil in a saucepan for 5 minutes. Add the lentils, red pepper and chicken broth and mix well. Simmer, covered, for 30 minutes. Add the black pepper, basil, oregano, tomato paste, vinegar and sugar and mix well. Simmer, uncovered, for 1 hour. Serve over spaghetti or other thin pasta.

♥ Note: See page 184 for the nutritional profile of this recipe.

Yield: 8 servings

Dr. Strong's Famous Spaghetti Sauce

3 medium onions, sliced
4 cloves of garlic, chopped
3 pounds ground turkey
2 tablespoons light butter
3 large jars Ragu spaghetti sauce
    with mushrooms
2 small cans tomato paste
3 bay leaves
1/2 to 1 teaspoon oregano
1/4 cup sugar
Salt to taste

Brown the onions and garlic in a nonstick skillet over low heat. Brown the turkey in the butter in a large saucepan over low heat, stirring until crumbly; drain. Add the spaghetti sauce, tomato paste, bay leaves, onion mixture, oregano and sugar and mix well. Simmer over medium heat for 3 hours, stirring frequently. Season with salt. Remove and discard the bay leaves. Serve over vermicelli or other thin pasta. Freezes well.

Yield: 12 servings

From the Heart

Vegetables and Side Dishes

"We don't stop playing because we grow old. We grow old because we stop playing." –Herbert Spencer

Kids Who Are Different

Here's to kids who are different,
The kids who don't always get A's,
The kids who have ears twice the size of their peers,
And noses that go on for days . . .
Here's to kids who are different,
The kids they call crazy or dumb,
The kids who don't fit, with the guts and the grit,
Who dance to a different drum . . .
Here's to the kids who are different,
The kids with the mischievous streak,
For when they have grown, as history's shown,
It's their difference that makes them unique.

—Digby Wolfe

ASPARAGUS WITH PISTACHIOS

¹/4 cup unsalted butter
2 tablespoons minced shallots
1 large tomato, seeded, chopped
1 tablespoon chopped fresh parsley
1 teaspoon fresh lemon juice
Salt and freshly ground pepper
*   to taste*
1 pound fresh asparagus, trimmed
¹/4 cup shelled roasted pistachios

Melt the butter in a large skillet over medium heat. Add the shallots. Sauté for 2 minutes. Add the tomato, parsley and lemon juice and mix well. Season with salt and pepper. Cook the asparagus in boiling salted water in a large saucepan for 2 minutes or until tender-crisp; drain well. Divide the asparagus evenly among individual plates. Spoon the sauce over the asparagus. Sprinkle with the pistachios.

Yield: 4 servings

GREEN BEAN BUNDLES

1 can whole green beans, drained
5 slices bacon, cut into halves
1 bottle French salad dressing

Divide the beans into 10 equal bundles. Wrap each bundle with 1 piece of bacon. Place in a casserole sprayed lightly with nonstick cooking spray. Pour the dressing over the bundles. Marinate in the refrigerator for several hours. Preheat the oven to 350 degrees. Bake for 30 minutes.

Yield: 2 to 4 servings

Carol's Baked Beans

1/4 cup sugar

1/4 cup packed brown sugar

1/4 cup barbecue sauce

1/4 cup catsup

2 tablespoons prepared mustard

2 tablespoons molasses

1 teaspoon chili powder

1 teaspoon salt

1/2 teaspoon pepper

1 (28-ounce) can pork and beans

1 (16-ounce) can kidney beans,
    drained

1 (16-ounce) can pinto beans,
    drained

1 (16-ounce) can black beans,
    drained

1 large onion, chopped

1 green bell pepper, chopped

8 ounces bacon, crisp-cooked,
    cut into 1-inch pieces

Preheat the oven to 350 degrees. Combine the sugar, brown sugar, barbecue sauce, catsup, mustard, molasses, chili powder, salt and pepper in a medium bowl and mix well. Mix all the beans, onion, green pepper and bacon in a large bowl. Add the sugar mixture and mix well. Spoon into a 2 1/2-quart casserole. Bake, covered, for 45 minutes. Bake, uncovered, for 15 minutes longer. May be kept warm in a 200-degree oven for up to 1 hour. Serve with barbecued ribs.

Yield: 16 to 20 servings

Kanto's Baked Beans

1 (15-ounce) can pineapple chunks
    in juice

1 (40-ounce) can pork and beans

1 (16-ounce) can green lima beans,
    drained

1 (15-ounce) can kidney beans,
    drained

1 cup catsup

1/3 cup packed brown sugar

1 tablespoon Dijon mustard

2 tablespoons Worcestershire sauce

2 tablespoons lemon juice

5 slices bacon, cut into 1-inch pieces

1 large onion, cut into wedges

1 green bell pepper, chopped

Preheat the oven to 300 degrees. Drain the pineapple, reserving 1/3 cup or more juice. Mix the beans, catsup, brown sugar, Dijon mustard, Worcestershire sauce, lemon juice, pineapple, reserved pineapple juice, bacon, onion and green pepper in a bowl. Spoon into a 3-quart baking dish. Bake for 3 hours. Freezes well.

Yield: 10 to 12 servings

Lentil Bobotie

3 tablespoons sunflower oil

2 onions, chopped

2 cups seeded peeled butternut
squash cubes

4 to 6 cloves of garlic, crushed

1/2 to 1 teaspoon chili paste

1 teaspoon medium-strength
curry powder

2 dried bay leaves

1 (14-ounce) can whole tomatoes

1 tablespoon ginger paste or freshly
grated gingerroot

24 sprigs of fresh coriander

2 teaspoons sugar

2 teaspoons salt, or to taste

Freshly ground pepper to taste

1 cup brown lentils, cooked

4 eggs

1 to 3 1/2 cups milk

1 cup rice

2 teaspoons turmeric

1 teaspoon salt

2 cinnamon sticks

1/2 cup raisins

2 tablespoons honey

2 tablespoons butter

Heat the oil in a large heavy skillet. Add the onions and squash. Sauté for 5 minutes or until the onions are translucent. Stir in the garlic, chili paste, curry powder and bay leaves. Add the undrained tomatoes. Sauté for 3 to 4 minutes or until heated through. Stir in the ginger paste, coriander and sugar. Season with 2 teaspoons salt and pepper. Simmer, covered, just until the squash is tender. Cook, uncovered, over high heat for 15 to 30 minutes or until most of the liquid has evaporated.

Remove and discard the bay leaves. Preheat the oven to 350 degrees. Alternate the lentils and squash mixture in a baking dish, beginning and ending with lentils. Beat the eggs into the milk; pour over the lentils. Bake for 45 to 50 minutes or until golden brown and set. Combine the rice, turmeric, 1 teaspoon salt and cinnamon with water to cover in a saucepan. Cook until the rice is tender and the water is absorbed. Remove and discard the cinnamon sticks. Stir the raisins, honey and butter into the rice. Serve the lentil mixture over the rice. Serve with mango chutney, yogurt, coconut, bananas and tomatoes.

Yield: 4 servings

BRUSSELS SPROUTS WITH MUSTARD SEEDS

2¹/2 pounds small fresh brussels
    sprouts
Salt to taste
¹/4 cup butter
2 tablespoons white mustard seeds
¹/4 cup grainy Dijon mustard
1 teaspoon salt
Freshly ground pepper to taste

Trim the brussels sprouts; make a cross cut in the base. Cook the brussels sprouts in boiling salted water in a large saucepan for 10 to 12 minutes or until tender-crisp; drain well. Combine the butter and mustard seeds in a large heavy skillet. Cook over medium heat until the butter is light brown, stirring constantly. Stir in the Dijon mustard and brussels sprouts. Season with 1 teaspoon salt and pepper. Cook for 2 to 3 minutes or until heated through, stirring constantly. Serve immediately. May substitute 1 tablespoon brown mustard seeds for 1 tablespoon of the white.

Yield: 12 servings

CARDAMOM CARROTS

1¹/2 cups water
³/4 teaspoon salt
2 pounds tiny carrots
1 teaspoon grated orange peel
¹/2 teaspoon ground cardamom
¹/4 cup packed brown sugar
¹/4 cup light margarine

Bring the water and salt to a boil in a saucepan. Add the carrots. Cook for 10 to 15 minutes or until tender; drain well. Add the orange peel, cardamom, brown sugar and margarine. Cook over low heat until heated through, stirring constantly.

Yield: 10 servings

CARROT AND BROCCOLI SOUFFLÉ

1 pound carrots
Salt to taste
2 tablespoons butter
Florets of 1 bunch broccoli
3 egg yolks
3 egg whites, stiffly beaten
Pepper to taste

Boil the carrots in salted water in a saucepan for 15 minutes or until tender; drain well. Purée in a food processor or blender. Combine the carrot purée and butter in a saucepan. Cook until the mixture is heated through and the butter is melted, stirring frequently; this will eliminate any remaining moisture. Simmer the broccoli in water to cover in a saucepan for 2 minutes; drain well. Preheat the oven to 325 degrees. Mix the carrot purée, broccoli, egg yolks, salt and pepper in a bowl. Fold in the egg whites. Spoon into a 1½-quart soufflé dish. Bake for 25 to 30 minutes or until heated through.

Yield: 8 to 10 servings

SCALLOPED EGGPLANT

1 large eggplant, cut into cubes
Salt to taste
⅓ cup milk
1 (10-ounce) can cream of
  mushroom soup
1 egg, lightly beaten
¾ cup herb-seasoned stuffing mix
½ cup chopped onion
½ cup herb-seasoned stuffing mix,
  finely crushed
2 tablespoons melted butter or
  margarine
1 cup shredded sharp Cheddar
  cheese

Preheat the oven to 350 degrees. Cook the eggplant in boiling salted water in a saucepan for 6 to 7 minutes or until tender; drain well. Stir the milk into the soup in a bowl. Blend in the egg. Add the eggplant, ¾ cup stuffing mix and onion and toss lightly to mix. Spoon into a greased 6x10x11-inch baking dish. Sprinkle with a mixture of ½ cup stuffing mix and butter. Top with the cheese. Bake for 20 minutes or until heated through.

Yield: 6 to 8 servings

Mushroom Casserole

6 slices bread, crusts trimmed,
    cubed
1 pound fresh mushrooms,
    sliced
¹/₂ cup chopped onion
¹/₂ cup chopped celery
¹/₄ cup butter
¹/₂ cup mayonnaise
1 teaspoon salt
¹/₂ teaspoon pepper
2 eggs, beaten
1 cup milk
1 cup canned cream of
    mushroom soup
¹/₂ cup shredded Cheddar cheese

Place half the bread cubes in a greased casserole. Sauté the mushrooms, onion and celery in the butter in a skillet. Add the mayonnaise, salt and pepper and mix well. Spread over the bread cubes. Top with the remaining bread. Pour a mixture of the eggs and milk over the top. Chill, covered, overnight. Spread the soup over the top. Bake for 50 minutes. Sprinkle with the cheese. Bake for 10 minutes. Recipe may be doubled and baked in a 9x13-inch casserole.

Yield: 8 to 10 servings

Things work out best

for those who make

the best of the way

things work out.

Potato Gnocchi

5 Idaho potatoes
2 egg yolks, at room temperature
1/2 teaspoon salt
1/4 teaspoon grated nutmeg
1/2 cup grated Parmesan cheese
1 1/2 cups flour
4 quarts boiling salted water
Tomato and Bell Pepper Sauce

Preheat the oven to 350 degrees. Pierce the potatoes several times with a fork. Bake for 1 hour or until tender. Peel and mash the potatoes. Mix the egg yolks, salt, nutmeg and cheese in a bowl. Add the mashed potatoes. Mix in enough of the flour gradually to make a soft dough. Roll small amounts of dough at a time into long cigar-shape 1 1/2-inch-diameter cylinders. Cut each cylinder into 1/2- to 1-inch pieces.

Drop the cylinders into the boiling salted water. Cook for 5 minutes or until the gnocchi float to the surface. Remove with a slotted spoon and drain well. Serve with Tomato and Bell Pepper Sauce.

Yield: 4 servings

Tomato and Bell Pepper Sauce

4 1/2 cups nonfat chicken broth
3 ounces sun-dried tomatoes, cut
    into 1/4-inch pieces
1 1/2 cups finely chopped roasted
    peeled red bell peppers
10 fresh plum tomatoes, cut into
    1/4-inch pieces
1 tablespoon minced fresh
    thyme leaves
1/2 teaspoon sugar
Salt and pepper to taste

Bring the chicken broth to a boil in a saucepan. Remove from the heat. Add the sun-dried tomatoes. Let stand, covered, for 20 to 30 minutes or until softened. Add the red peppers and plum tomatoes. Simmer over medium heat for 5 minutes. Stir in the thyme, sugar, salt and pepper.

Hash Brown Potato Casserole

1 (10-ounce) can cream of
    chicken soup
2 cups sour cream
8 ounces sharp New York Cheddar
    cheese, shredded
1/2 cup melted butter
1/2 cup chopped onion
1 (2-pound) package frozen hash
    brown potatoes, partially
    thawed
Salt and pepper to taste

Preheat the oven to 375 degrees.
Mix the soup, sour cream and
cheese in a medium bowl. Add
the butter and onion and mix
well. Add the potatoes and
mix well. Season with salt and
pepper. Spoon into a baking
dish. Bake for 45 minutes.

Yield: 8 to 10 servings

Blender Potato Kugel

6 potatoes, cut into cubes
3 eggs
1 onion, cut into pieces
1 1/2 teaspoons salt
1/8 teaspoon pepper
2 tablespoons matzo meal
2 tablespoons corn or peanut oil

Preheat the oven to 350 degrees.
Combine 2 of the potatoes, 1
egg and some of the onion in a
blender container. Process until
mixed. Add some of the salt and
pepper. Pour into a large bowl.
Repeat with the remaining
potatoes, eggs, onion, salt and
pepper. Add the matzo meal to
the potato mixture and mix well.
Heat the oil in a 1 1/2-quart baking
dish. Spoon the potato mixture
into the dish. Bake for 45 to 60
minutes or until the potatoes
are tender and the mixture is
heated through.

Yield: 8 servings

Yellow Squash Soufflé

1/4 cup butter or margarine

5 cans yellow squash, drained, or
   2 pounds fresh yellow squash,
   cooked

2 eggs, beaten

1/2 cup mayonnaise

1/4 cup chopped green onions

1/4 cup chopped green bell pepper

2/3 cup shredded sharp Cheddar
   cheese

1 tablespoon chopped pimento

1 teaspoon salt

1/2 teaspoon pepper

1 teaspoon sugar

Buttered cracker crumbs

Preheat the oven to 350 degrees. Melt the butter in a 2-quart casserole. Combine the butter, squash, eggs, mayonnaise, green onions, green pepper, cheese, pimento, salt, pepper and sugar in a bowl and mix well. Spoon into the casserole. Top with the cracker crumbs. Bake for 35 to 40 minutes or until heated through.

Yield: 8 servings

If I can stop one heart from breaking, I shall not live in vain. If I can ease one life the aching, or cool one pain, or help one fainting robin into his nest again, I shall not live in vain.

—Emily Dickinson

Spinach Zucchini Boats

1 (10-ounce) package frozen
    chopped spinach
3 zucchini
2 tablespoons flour
1/2 cup milk
1/3 cup shredded Cheddar cheese
4 slices bacon, crisp-cooked,
    crumbled
Bread crumbs
Butter

Preheat the oven to 350 degrees. Cook the spinach using the package directions; drain well. Cook the zucchini in boiling water in a saucepan for 10 minutes; drain well. Cut the zucchini into halves lengthwise. Scoop out and chop the zucchini pulp, leaving the shells intact. Reserve the shells. Mix the zucchini pulp with the spinach. Blend the flour and milk in a saucepan. Add the spinach mixture. Cook until thick, stirring frequently. Add the cheese and bacon and mix well. Fill the reserved zucchini shells with the spinach mixture. Top with bread crumbs and dot with butter. Place on a baking sheet. Bake for 20 minutes.

Yield: 6 servings

Crusty Tomatoes

6 tablespoons melted butter
1/2 cup herb-seasoned stuffing mix
1/2 cup grated Parmesan cheese
4 firm medium tomatoes, cored,
    cut into halves
Dijon mustard
Salt and pepper to taste

Preheat the oven to 350 degrees. Mix the butter, stuffing mix and cheese in a bowl. Spread the cut sides of the tomatoes with a small amount of Dijon mustard. Sprinkle with salt and pepper. Spoon an equal portion of the cheese mixture on top of each tomato half. Place in a greased 9x13-inch glass baking dish. Bake for 15 to 20 minutes or until the tomatoes are cooked through and the tops are crusty.

Yield: 8 servings

Sweet Potato Casserole

3 cups mashed cooked sweet
   potatoes
1/2 cup sugar
2 eggs, beaten
1/4 cup melted margarine
1/2 cup milk
1 1/2 teaspoons vanilla extract
1/2 teaspoon nutmeg
1/2 teaspoon cinnamon
1/2 cup packed brown sugar
1/2 cup crushed cornflakes
1 cup chopped pecans
1/4 cup melted margarine

Preheat the oven to 325 degrees. Combine the sweet potatoes, sugar, eggs, 1/4 cup margarine, milk, vanilla extract, nutmeg and cinnamon in a bowl and mix well. Spoon into a shallow 1 1/2-quart baking dish. Mix the brown sugar, cornflakes, pecans and 1/4 cup margarine in a bowl. Spread over the sweet potato mixture. Bake for 35 minutes. May omit the milk and add 1/2 cup orange juice and grated peel of 1 orange; bake for 30 minutes and then top with marshmallows instead of the brown sugar mixture; bake for 5 minutes longer or until the marshmallows are puffed and beginning to brown.

Yield: 6 to 8 servings

When you get into a tight place and everything goes against you, till it seems as though you could not hold on a minute longer, never give up then, for that is just the place and time that the tide will turn.

—Harriet Beecher Stowe

Black Beans and Rice

1 (16-ounce) package black beans

6 cups water, or 5 cups water and
1 cup dry white wine

2 medium carrots, chopped

1/2 large white onion, chopped

1 rib celery, chopped

1 cup chopped trimmed smoked
ham

2 tablespoons lime juice

1 tablespoon salt

2 drops of liquid smoke

1 tablespoon Worcestershire sauce

2 tablespoons Pica-Peppa Sauce

1 tablespoon Creole seasoning

3 cloves of garlic, pressed

2 canned jalapeños, chopped

1 tablespoon celery flakes

1/4 cup white vinegar

Hot sauce to taste

Cooked yellow rice

Sour cream

Sort and rinse the beans. Soak the beans overnight in water to cover; drain and rinse. Combine the beans, 6 cups water, carrots, onion, celery, ham, lime juice, salt, liquid smoke, Worcestershire sauce, Pica-Peppa sauce, Creole seasoning, garlic, jalapeños and celery flakes and mix well. Bring to a boil; reduce the heat. Simmer, covered, for 4 to 6 hours or until the beans are tender, adding additional water if needed.

Simmer, uncovered, until thickened; mash some of the beans with a spoon or whisk if further thickening is desired. Stir in the vinegar and hot sauce. Serve over rice. Top each serving with a dollop of sour cream. Garnish with chopped scallions and red bell pepper.

Yield: 8 to 12 servings

GREEN RICE

3/4 cup minced green onions

3 tablespoons olive oil

2 cups chicken broth

1 cup rice

1/4 cup minced parsley

1 teaspoon salt

1/4 teaspoon pepper

1 can mushrooms

Preheat the oven to 350 degrees. Cook the green onions in the oil in a skillet until tender. Add the chicken broth, rice, parsley, salt, pepper and mushrooms and mix well. Spoon into a 2-quart baking dish. Bake, covered, for 30 minutes. Toss lightly before serving.

Yield: 6 servings

LEMON RICE

2 tablespoons unsalted butter

1 tablespoon olive oil

1 small onion, finely chopped

1 cup long grain rice

1 3/4 cups chicken broth

1/4 cup fresh lemon juice

1 2/3 teaspoons freshly grated lemon peel

1/2 teaspoon salt, or to taste

1/4 teaspoon freshly ground pepper, or to taste

Preheat the oven to 350 degrees. Heat the butter and oil in a small skillet. Add the onion. Sauté over medium heat for 5 minutes or until tender and translucent. Add the rice, stirring to coat. Add the chicken broth, lemon juice, lemon peel, salt and pepper and mix well. Bring to a boil. Spoon into a small casserole. Bake, covered, for 25 to 30 minutes or until the liquid is absorbed and the rice is tender. Serve hot, garnished with freshly chopped parsley and freshly grated lemon peel.

Yield: 4 servings

Rice Pulao

1½ cups long grain rice, rinsed

2½ cups cold water

2 tablespoons butter or margarine

4 whole black peppercorns

4 whole cloves

1 cinnamon stick, cut into pieces

¼ teaspoon cumin seeds

Salt to taste

½ teaspoon turmeric powder

1 (10-ounce) package frozen peas

¼ cup raisins (optional)

½ cup sautéed or roasted whole
    cashews or peanuts (optional)

Soak the rice in the cold water for 30 minutes. Melt the butter in a 2-quart saucepan. Drop in the peppercorns, cloves, cinnamon pieces and cumin seeds. Sauté for 2 minutes. Add the salt and turmeric. Add the undrained rice and mix well. Bring to a boil; reduce the heat to low. Stir through the mixture once. Cook, covered, until ¾ of the water is absorbed. Add the peas, raisins and nuts and mix gently. Cook until all the water is absorbed and the rice is tender. Remove the cloves, peppercorns and cinnamon pieces before serving.

Yield: 4 servings

The best way to cheer yourself up is to cheer everybody else up.

—Mark Twain

Blintz Casserole

1 cup melted butter

1/2 cup sugar

2 eggs

1/4 cup milk

1 teaspoon vanilla extract

1 cup sifted flour

1/8 teaspoon salt

1 tablespoon baking powder

2 pounds cottage cheese

2 eggs, beaten

1/4 cup sugar

1/8 teaspoon salt

1 teaspoon vanilla extract

Juice of 1 lemon

Preheat the oven to 325 degrees. For the batter, cream the butter and 1/2 cup sugar in a mixer bowl until light and fluffy. Add 2 eggs, milk, 1 teaspoon vanilla extract, flour, 1/8 teaspoon salt and baking powder and mix well. For the filling, combine the cottage cheese, 2 eggs, 1/4 cup sugar, 1/8 teaspoon salt, 1 teaspoon vanilla extract and lemon juice in a bowl and mix well. Place half the batter in a greased 9x13-inch casserole. Spread with the filling. Top with the remaining batter. Bake for 1 to 1 1/2 hours or until set. May serve as a vegetarian entrée. May top with canned pie filling.

Yield: 8 to 10 servings

Deluxe Macaroni and Cheese

1 (8-ounce) package elbow macaroni

2 cups cream-style cottage cheese

1 cup sour cream

1 egg, lightly beaten

3/4 teaspoon salt

1/8 teaspoon pepper

2 cups shredded sharp cheese

Paprika to taste

Preheat the oven to 350 degrees. Cook the macaroni using the package directions; drain and rinse. Combine the cottage cheese, sour cream, egg, salt, pepper and cheese in a large bowl and mix well. Add the macaroni and mix well. Spoon into a greased 2-quart casserole. Sprinkle with paprika. Bake for 45 minutes.

Yield: 8 to 10 servings

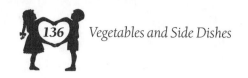
ℬAKED ℭURRIED ℱRUIT

1 (16-ounce) can pineapple chunks
1 cup packed light brown sugar
1 tablespoon curry
1/4 cup spiced rum
1 (20-ounce) can sliced peaches,
 drained
1 (20-ounce) can pears, drained,
 sliced
1 (17-ounce) can pitted dark
 cherries, drained
1/2 cup sliced almonds
24 macaroons or coconut cookies,
 crumbled
1/2 cup butter

Drain the pineapple, reserving the juice. Mix the brown sugar, curry, rum and reserved juice in a bowl and set aside. Place the pineapple, peaches, pears and cherries in a 9x13-inch casserole. Pour the juice mixture over the fruit. Sprinkle with the almonds. Top with the cookie crumbs and dot with the butter. Chill, covered tightly with plastic wrap, overnight. Preheat the oven to 350 degrees. Bake, uncovered, for 30 minutes.

Yield: 8 servings

We would never learn

to be brave and patient

if there were only joy

in the world.

—Helen Keller

Sweethearts

Desserts

"When love and skill work together, expect a masterpiece." –*John Ruskin*

I asked God for strength that I might achieve
I was made weak that I might learn humbly to obey.
I asked for health that I might do greater things
I was given infirmity that I might do better things.
I asked for riches that I might be happy
I was given poverty that I might be wise.
I asked for power that I might have the praise of men
I was given weakness that I might feel the need of God.
I asked for all things that I might enjoy life
I was given life that I might enjoy all things.
I got nothing I asked for but everything I hoped for
Almost despite myself my unspoken prayers were answered.
I am among all men, most richly blessed.

—Unknown soldier

Black Beast Cake

¹/₂ cup water

1 cup sugar

8 ounces unsweetened chocolate

4 ounces semisweet chocolate

*1 cup room temperature unsalted
    butter, cut into small pieces*

*5 extra-large eggs, at room
    temperature*

¹/₃ cup sugar

Sherried Whipped Cream

Preheat the oven to 350 degrees. Butter a 9-inch springform pan and line with waxed paper; butter the waxed paper. Combine the water and 1 cup sugar in a heavy saucepan. Boil for 4 minutes or until the mixture reaches 220 degrees on a candy thermometer. Remove from the heat. Add the unsweetened chocolate and semisweet chocolate, stirring until melted and smooth. Add the butter 1 or 2 pieces at a time, stirring until smooth and blended. Beat the eggs and ¹/₃ cup sugar at high speed in a mixer bowl for 15 minutes or until tripled in volume.

Fold in the chocolate mixture gently; overstirring will cause air bubbles in the cake. Spoon into the prepared pan. Set the springform pan in a larger pan of boiling water deep enough to come ³/₄ inch up the side of the springform pan. Bake for 30 minutes or until a knife inserted near the center comes out clean. Cool in the pan. Chill overnight. Serve with Sherried Whipped Cream.

Yield: 12 to 16 servings

Sherried Whipped Cream

1 pint whipping cream, chilled

¹/₄ cup confectioners' sugar

¹/₄ cup dry sherry

Beat the whipping cream in a cold mixer bowl with cold beaters until soft peaks form. Add the confectioners' sugar gradually, beating constantly until stiff peaks form. Beat in the sherry.

Mom's Apple Cake

3 to 4 apples, peeled, sliced
3 to 4 teaspoons cinnamon
3 to 4 tablespoons sugar
3 cups sifted flour
1 tablespoon baking powder
1/2 teaspoon salt
1/3 cup orange juice
2 1/2 teaspoons vanilla extract
1 cup vegetable oil
4 eggs
2 1/4 cups sugar
Confectioners' sugar

Preheat the oven to 350 degrees. Mix the apples, cinnamon and 3 to 4 tablespoons sugar in a small bowl. Sift the flour, baking powder and salt together. Mix the orange juice, vanilla extract and oil in a medium bowl. Cream the eggs and 2 1/4 cups sugar in a mixer bowl until light and fluffy. Add the flour mixture and orange juice mixture alternately to the creamed mixture, beating well after each addition. Alternate layers of the batter and apple mixture in a greased bundt pan. Bake for 1 3/4 hours. Cool in the pan. Invert onto a serving plate. Sprinkle with confectioners' sugar.

Yield: 12 to 16 servings

Mississippi Mud Cake

4 eggs
1 1/2 cups flour
2 cups sugar
1/8 teaspoon salt
1 cup margarine
1/2 cup baking cocoa
1 1/2 cups chopped pecans
1 package miniature marshmallows
Chocolate Frosting

Preheat the oven to 325 degrees. Mix the eggs, flour, sugar and salt in a large bowl. Melt the margarine and cocoa in a saucepan, stirring frequently. Add to the flour mixture and mix well. Stir in the pecans. Spoon into a nonstick 9x13-inch cake pan. Bake for 30 minutes or until the cake tests done. Top the hot cake with the marshmallows. Cool in the pan. Spread with Chocolate Frosting.

Yield: 15 to 18 servings

Anna's Coca-Cola Cake

Chocolate Frosting

1/4 cup butter
1/3 cup baking cocoa
1 (1-pound) package confectioners'
    sugar
1/8 teaspoon salt
1 teaspoon vanilla extract
1/3 cup (about) milk

Heat the butter and cocoa in a saucepan until the butter is melted, stirring frequently. Pour into a large bowl. Beat in the confectioners' sugar. Stir in the salt, vanilla extract and enough milk to make of spreading consistency.

1 cup margarine, softened
3 tablespoons baking cocoa
2 cups flour
1 3/4 cups sugar
1 teaspoon baking soda
2 eggs
1 teaspoon vanilla extract
1/2 cup buttermilk
1 cup Coca-Cola
2 cups miniature marshmallows
Coca-Cola Frosting (optional)

Preheat the oven to 350 degrees. Combine the margarine, cocoa, flour, sugar, baking soda, eggs, vanilla extract and buttermilk in a mixer bowl. Beat at medium speed for 1 minute. Add the Coca-Cola and mix well. Stir in the marshmallows. Spoon into a greased and floured 9x13-inch cake pan. Bake for 45 minutes. Cool in the pan. Spread with Coca-Cola Frosting.

Yield: 15 to 18 servings

Coca-Cola Frosting

1/2 cup margarine, softened
3 tablespoons baking cocoa
1/3 cup Coca-Cola
4 cups confectioners' sugar

Combine the margarine, cocoa and Coca-Cola in a bowl and mix well. Add the confectioners' sugar, beating until of spreading consistency.

Orange-Filled Coconut Cake

3 cups sifted cake flour

2¼ teaspoons baking powder

¼ teaspoon salt

1 cup shortening

2 cups sugar

½ teaspoon almond extract

4 eggs

1 cup milk

Orange Filling

Coconut Frosting

Flaked coconut (optional)

Grated orange peel (optional)

Preheat the oven to 375 degrees. Grease three 9-inch round cake pans and line with waxed paper. Sift the flour, baking powder and salt together. Cream the shortening and sugar in a mixer bowl until light and fluffy. Stir in the almond extract. Beat in the eggs 1 at a time. Add the flour mixture and milk alternately, beating well after each addition. Divide the batter evenly among the cake pans. Bake for 25 minutes or until the layers test done. Cool in the pans for 5 minutes. Remove to a wire rack to cool completely. Spread Orange Filling between the layers. Spread Coconut Frosting between the layers and over the top and side of the cake. Sprinkle with coconut and orange peel.

Note: Orange-Filled Coconut Cake is pictured on the cover.

Yield: 12 servings

Orange Filling

½ cup cake flour

1 cup sugar

¼ teaspoon salt

¼ cup water

1¼ cups orange juice

¼ cup lemon juice

2 tablespoons grated orange peel

Grated peel of 1 lemon

4 egg yolks, lightly beaten

Mix the flour, sugar and salt in a heavy saucepan. Add the water, stirring until smooth. Add the orange juice, lemon juice, orange peel and lemon peel. Cook over low heat until the mixture is thick and almost translucent, stirring occasionally. Add a small amount of the hot mixture to the egg yolks; add the egg yolks to the hot mixture gradually, stirring constantly. Cook over low heat for 5 minutes or until thick, stirring frequently. Let cool.

Mama's Cream Cheese Pound Cake

Coconut Frosting

1½ cups sugar

½ teaspoon cream of tartar

⅛ teaspoon salt

½ cup hot water

½ cup stiffly beaten egg whites

¼ teaspoon almond extract

2 cups grated fresh coconut

Combine the sugar, cream of tartar, salt and hot water in a saucepan and mix well. Cook without stirring to 240 degrees on a candy thermometer, soft-ball stage. Add the syrup gradually to the egg whites in a mixer bowl, beating constantly at high speed. Add the almond extract. Stir in the coconut.

1½ cups butter, softened

3 cups sugar

8 ounces cream cheese, softened

6 eggs

3 cups cake flour

½ teaspoon salt

1 teaspoon vanilla extract

1 teaspoon lemon extract

Caramel Icing (optional)

Preheat the oven to 325 degrees. Cream the butter, sugar and cream cheese in a mixer bowl until light and fluffy. Beat in the eggs 1 at a time. Add the flour 1 cup at a time, beating just until mixed; do not overbeat. Stir in the salt, vanilla extract and lemon extract. Spoon into a greased and floured tube pan. Bake for 1¼ hours or until a wooden pick inserted near the center comes out clean. Cool in the pan for several minutes. Invert onto a serving plate. Spread Caramel Icing over the top and side of the cake.

Yield: 16 servings

Caramel Icing

½ cup sugar

1 cup butter

1 cup evaporated milk

2½ cups sugar

2 teaspoons vanilla extract

Place ½ cup sugar in a large cast-iron skillet over medium heat. Cook until the sugar dissolves and caramelizes, stirring frequently. At the same time, bring the butter, evaporated milk and 2½ cups sugar to a boil in a heavy saucepan over medium heat, stirring constantly. Add the caramelized sugar, stirring until blended and smooth. Boil until the mixture reaches 234 to 240 degrees on a candy thermometer, soft-ball stage. Remove from the heat. Stir in the vanilla extract. Place the pan in cold water. Beat the mixture until cooled and of spreading consistency; stir in a few drops of hot water if the mixture hardens too much.

Piña Colada Cake

1 (2-layer) package pudding-recipe
   yellow cake mix
1 can sweetened condensed milk
1 can liquid piña colada mix
16 ounces whipped topping
1 cup shredded fresh frozen coconut
   (optional)
8 pineapple slices (optional)
8 maraschino cherries (optional)

Prepare and bake the cake mix using the package directions for a 9x13-inch glass baking dish. Pierce the hot cake several times with a fork. Combine the condensed milk and piña colada mix in a bowl and mix well with a fork. Pour slowly over the cake, allowing the mixture to seep into the cake. Cool to room temperature. Spread with the whipped topping. Sprinkle with the coconut. Top with the pineapple and cherries. Chill, covered, overnight. Serve from the baking dish.

Yield: 12 to 15 servings

Faith is continuing to run the race, assured that you will get your second wind.

Poppy Seed Cakes

3 cups flour
1/2 teaspoon salt
1 1/2 teaspoons baking powder
3 eggs
1 cup vegetable oil
2 1/4 cups sugar
1 1/2 cups milk
1 1/2 tablespoons poppy seeds
1 1/2 teaspoons almond extract
1 1/2 teaspoons vanilla extract
1 1/2 teaspoons butter flavoring
Orange Glaze

Preheat the oven to 350 degrees. Combine the flour, salt, baking powder, eggs, oil, sugar, milk, poppy seeds, almond extract, vanilla extract and butter flavoring in a bowl and mix well. Spoon into 2 greased loaf pans, 3 small loaf pans or 6 miniature loaf pans. Bake for 1 hour. The top of the loaves will crack. Cool in the pans. Remove to serving plates. Pour Orange Glaze over the tops, using a knife to bring glaze drips back to the top. Freezes well.

Yield: 20 to 24 servings

Orange Glaze

1/4 cup orange juice
1/2 teaspoon almond extract
1/2 teaspoon vanilla extract
1/2 teaspoon butter flavoring
3/4 cup confectioners' sugar

Mix the orange juice, almond extract, vanilla extract and butter flavoring in a bowl. Add the confectioners' sugar, mixing until of glaze consistency.

Zinfandel Cake

1 (2-layer) package vanilla
  cake mix
1 small package French vanilla
  instant pudding mix
1/2 cup white zinfandel
1/2 cup vegetable oil
4 eggs
1/2 cup water
Zinfandel Topping
Unsalted almonds
Confectioners' sugar

Preheat the oven to 350 degrees.
Combine the cake mix, pudding
mix, wine, oil, eggs and water in
a bowl and mix well. Spoon into
a greased bundt pan. Bake for
50 to 60 minutes or until the
cake tests done. Cool in the pan.
Invert onto a serving plate.
Baste with Zinfandel Topping.
Sprinkle with almonds and
confectioners' sugar.

Yield: 12 servings

Zinfandel Topping

1/4 cup water
1/4 cup white zinfandel
1/4 cup sugar
1/4 cup butter

Combine the water, wine, sugar
and butter in a saucepan. Cook
over low heat for 2 to 3 minutes
or until the butter melts, stirring
constantly.

Hannah's Chocolate Fudge Cookies

1 (2-layer) package devil's food
  cake mix
1/2 cup vegetable oil
2 eggs
1 cup semisweet chocolate chips
1/2 cup chopped pecans (optional)

Preheat the oven to 350 degrees.
Combine the cake mix, oil and
eggs in a mixer bowl. Beat at
medium speed until blended.
Stir in the chocolate chips and
pecans. Drop by rounded
teaspoonfuls 2 inches apart onto
nonstick cookie sheets. Bake
for 10 minutes for soft chewy
cookies or longer for crispy
cookies. Cool on the cookie
sheets for 5 minutes. Remove
to wire racks to cool completely.
Use yellow cake mix and chocolate
chips for chocolate chip cookies;
confetti cake mix for sugar
cookies; lemon cake mix for
lemon sugar cookies; or use
devil's food cake mix with
Reese's chips.

Yield: 3 dozen

Hillary Clinton's Chocolate Chip Cookies

1½ cups flour

1 teaspoon salt

1 teaspoon baking soda

1 cup shortening

½ cup sugar

1 cup packed light brown sugar

1 teaspoon vanilla extract

2 eggs

2 cups rolled oats

2 cups semisweet chocolate chips

Preheat the oven to 350 degrees. Mix the flour, salt and baking soda together. Cream the shortening, sugar, brown sugar and vanilla extract in a large mixer bowl. Add the eggs, beating until light and fluffy. Add the flour mixture and oats gradually, beating well after each addition. Stir in the chocolate chips. Drop by rounded teaspoonfuls onto greased cookie sheets. Bake for 8 to 10 minutes or until golden brown. Cool on the cookie sheets on wire racks for 2 minutes. Remove the cookies to wire racks to cool completely.

Yield: 2 dozen

The surest cure for loneliness, the quickest way to happiness is found in this, a simple creed: go serve someone in greater need.

Georgia Brownies

1½ cups flour
2 cups sugar
10 tablespoons baking cocoa
1 teaspoon salt
1 cup shortening, or
   ½ cup margarine and
   ½ cup shortening
4 eggs, beaten
1 teaspoon vanilla extract
1 cup chopped pecans or walnuts
Fudge Frosting

Preheat the oven to 350 degrees. Combine the flour, sugar, cocoa, salt, shortening, eggs, vanilla extract and pecans in a bowl and mix well. Spread in a greased 9x13-inch baking pan. Bake for 25 to 30 minutes or until a wooden pick inserted near the center comes out clean. Pour Fudge Frosting over the warm brownies.

Yield: 1½ to 2 dozen

Fudge Frosting

2 cups sugar
½ cup baking cocoa
½ cup evaporated milk
3 tablespoons butter

Combine the sugar, cocoa, evaporated milk and butter in a saucepan. Bring to a rolling boil. Cook for 1 to 2 minutes or until the butter melts, stirring constantly. Remove from the heat. Beat just until the mixture begins to thicken.

Trust in the Lord with all thine heart, and lean not unto thine own understanding. In all thy ways acknowledge Him, and He shall direct thy paths.

—Proverbs 3:5-6

One-Bowl Low-Fat Brownies

4 ounces unsweetened chocolate

2 cups sugar

Egg substitute equivalent to 3 eggs

2 teaspoons vanilla extract

1/2 (4-ounce) jar baby food
　　applesauce

1 cup flour

Preheat the oven to 350 degrees. Place the chocolate in a large microwave-safe bowl. Microwave on High for 2 minutes or until melted. Stir until smooth. Beat the sugar into the chocolate. Beat in the egg substitute and vanilla extract. Beat in the applesauce and flour. Spread in a greased 9x9-inch baking pan. Bake for 30 to 35 minutes or until a knife inserted near the center comes out with fudgy crumbs; do not overbake. Cool in the pan. Cut into squares. May add 1 cup chopped pecans or walnuts. May be baked at 325 degrees in a glass baking dish.

♥ *Note:* See page 184 for the nutritional profile of this recipe.

Yield: 1 dozen

Chocolate Bar Cookies

1 cup butter or margarine, softened

1 cup packed brown sugar

1 teaspoon vanilla extract

2 cups self-rising flour

2 (7-ounce) chocolate bars, broken
　　into pieces

1/2 package Heath bits (optional)

Preheat the oven to 350 degrees. Mix the butter and brown sugar in a bowl. Stir in the vanilla extract. Add the flour and mix well. Press into a 10x15-inch cookie sheet with sides. Bake for 15 minutes. Place the chocolate over the baked layer. Bake for 2 minutes or until the chocolate is soft. Spread the chocolate to the edges. Sprinkle with Heath bits. Let stand until the chocolate is set. Cut into bars.

Yield: 4 dozen

Bubbie Ida's Oatmeal Cookies

1 cup flour
1/2 teaspoon baking powder
1/2 teaspoon baking soda
1/4 teaspoon salt
1/2 cup sugar
1/2 cup packed brown sugar
1/2 cup vegetable oil
1 egg
1/4 teaspoon vanilla extract
3/4 cup quick-cooking oats
1 cup raisins
Cinnamon
Sugar

Sift the flour, baking powder, baking soda and salt into a large bowl. Mix 1/2 cup sugar, brown sugar, oil, egg and vanilla extract in a medium bowl. Add to the flour mixture and mix well. Add the oats and raisins and mix well. Chill for several hours. Preheat the oven to 350 degrees. Shape the dough into tablespoon-size balls. Roll the balls in a mixture of cinnamon and sugar. Place on a nonstick cookie sheet. Bake for 8 to 10 minutes or until brown. Cool on the cookie sheet for 1 minute. Remove to a wire rack to cool completely.

Note: Bubbie Ida's Oatmeal Cookies are pictured on the cover.

Yield: 3 dozen

Persimmon Cookies

2 cups flour
1 teaspoon baking soda
1/2 teaspoon cinnamon
1/2 teaspoon ground cloves
1/2 teaspoon nutmeg
1/8 teaspoon salt
1/2 cup butter, softened
1 cup sugar
1 egg
1 cup persimmon pulp
1 cup chopped dates
1 cup chopped pecans or walnuts

Preheat the oven to 350 degrees. Sift the flour, baking soda, cinnamon, cloves, nutmeg and salt together 3 times. Cream the butter and sugar in a mixer bowl until light and fluffy. Add the egg and persimmon and mix well. Add the flour mixture gradually, mixing well after each addition. Mix in the dates and pecans. Drop by spoonfuls onto a nonstick cookie sheet. Bake for 15 minutes.

Yield: 2 dozen

Orange Slice Cookies

1¹/₂ cups flour

¹/₂ teaspoon baking soda

¹/₂ teaspoon baking powder

¹/₂ teaspoon salt

²/₃ cup butter, softened

²/₃ cup sugar

²/₃ cup packed brown sugar

1 egg

1 teaspoon vanilla extract

1¹/₂ cups quick-cooking oats

1 cup flaked coconut

1¹/₂ cups cut-up pieces orange
    candy slices

Preheat the oven to 375 degrees. Sift the flour, baking soda, baking powder and salt together. Cream the butter, sugar and brown sugar in a mixer bowl until light and fluffy. Add the egg and vanilla extract and mix well. Add the flour mixture, oats and coconut and mix well. Stir in the candy. Shape into small balls. Place on a greased cookie sheet. Bake for 10 to 12 minutes or until brown.

Yield: 1¹/₂ to 2 dozen

What we call adversity,

God calls opportunity.

What we call tribulation,

God calls growth.

LEMON FROST PIE WITH BLUEBERRY SAUCE

1 cup flour
2 tablespoons sugar
1/4 teaspoon salt
1/2 cup margarine
2 egg whites, at room temperature
2/3 cup sugar
2 teaspoons freshly grated
   lemon peel
1/4 cup fresh lemon juice
2 to 3 drops of yellow food coloring
   (optional)
1 cup whipping cream, whipped
Blueberry Sauce

Preheat the oven to 375 degrees. Combine the flour, 2 tablespoons sugar and salt in a bowl. Cut in the margarine until crumbly. Press over the bottom and up the side of a 9-inch pie plate. Bake for 12 to 15 minutes or until brown. Beat the egg whites in a large mixer bowl until soft peaks form. Add 2/3 cup sugar gradually, beating constantly until stiff peaks form. Add the lemon peel, lemon juice and food coloring and mix gently. Fold in the whipped cream. Spoon into the prepared crust. Chill until serving time. Serve with hot or cold Blueberry Sauce. May be prepared up to 2 days ahead and stored in the refrigerator. May be frozen; thaw before serving.

Yield: 8 servings

Blueberry Sauce

2 tablespoons cornstarch
2/3 cup cold water
2/3 cup sugar
1 teaspoon fresh lemon juice
1/8 teaspoon salt
2 cups fresh or frozen blueberries

Dissolve the cornstarch in the water in a medium saucepan. Add the sugar, lemon juice and salt. Cook over medium heat until thick, stirring constantly and adding additional water if needed. Add the blueberries and mix gently. May be prepared ahead and stored in the refrigerator until serving time.

Key Lime Pie

2 cups sour cream
1 can sweetened condensed milk
2¹/₂ ounces bottled or fresh
    Key lime juice
1 graham cracker pie shell
Whipped topping

Mix the sour cream, condensed milk and lime juice in a bowl. Spoon into the pie shell. Chill thoroughly. Spread with whipped topping.

Yield: 8 servings

Kahlúa Pecan Pie

1 recipe (1-crust) pie pastry
¹/₄ cup butter, softened
³/₄ cup sugar
1 teaspoon vanilla extract
2 tablespoons flour
3 eggs
¹/₂ cup Kahlúa
¹/₂ cup dark corn syrup
³/₄ cup evaporated milk
1 cup whole or chopped pecans
¹/₂ cup whipping cream, whipped
    (optional)
Pecan halves (optional)

Fit the pastry into a 9-inch pie plate. Chill thoroughly. Preheat the oven to 400 degrees. Cream the butter, sugar, vanilla extract and flour in a mixer bowl until light and fluffy. Beat in the eggs 1 at a time. Stir in the Kahlúa, corn syrup, evaporated milk and whole pecans. Spoon into the prepared pie plate. Bake for 10 minutes. Reduce the oven temperature to 325 degrees. Bake for 40 minutes or until the center is set. Chill until serving time. Top with whipped cream and pecan halves.

Note: Kahlúa Pecan Pie is pictured on the cover.

Yield: 8 to 10 servings

"No Name" Pie

6 egg whites
2 cups sugar
48 butter crackers, finely crushed
2 cups chopped pecans
2 cups whipping cream, whipped,
   or 2 cups whipped topping
6 tablespoons Nestlé Quik

Preheat the oven to 350 degrees. Beat the egg whites in a mixer bowl until stiff peaks form. Fold in the sugar. Add the cracker crumbs and pecans and mix gently. Spoon into a lightly greased 3-quart casserole. Bake for 30 minutes. Let cool. Mix the whipped cream and Nestlé Quik in a bowl. Spread in the cooled crust. Chill for 2 hours or longer. Garnish with additional whipped cream and a maraschino cherry.

Yield: 15 servings

Chocolate Eclair Dessert

2 tablespoons milk
1/4 cup butter
2 tablespoons baking cocoa
1/2 cup sugar
1 small package French vanilla
   instant pudding mix
1 1/2 cups milk
4 ounces whipped topping
1/2 package graham crackers

Combine 2 tablespoons milk, butter, cocoa and sugar in a saucepan. Boil for 1 minute. Set aside to cool. Combine the pudding mix and 1 1/2 cups milk in a bowl, beating until thickened. Fold in the whipped topping. Alternate layers of the graham crackers and pudding in a 9x13-inch dish, beginning and ending with graham crackers. Spread with the cocoa mixture. Best when prepared 1 day ahead and stored in the refrigerator.

Yield: 15 to 18 servings

Baked Fudge

4 eggs
2 cups sugar
1/2 cup flour
1/2 cup baking cocoa
1 cup melted margarine or butter
1 cup chopped walnuts
13/4 teaspoons vanilla extract
1/4 teaspoon salt
Whipped cream

Preheat the oven to 425 degrees. Beat the eggs in a mixer bowl until pale yellow. Add the sugar, flour, cocoa, margarine, walnuts, vanilla extract and salt and mix well. Spoon into an 8x12-inch baking pan. Place in a larger pan filled with enough water to reach partway up the sides of the baking pan. Bake for 45 to 50 minutes or until set. Serve warm with whipped cream.

Yield: 6 to 8 servings

Saltine Bark

1 sleeve saltines
1 cup butter
1 cup sugar
1 teaspoon vanilla extract
2 cups chocolate chips

Preheat the oven to 350 degrees. Place a single layer of crackers on a foil-lined baking sheet. Combine the butter and sugar in a saucepan. Boil for 3 minutes. Add the vanilla extract and mix well. Pour over the crackers. Bake for 6 to 8 minutes or until brown; do not overbake. Sprinkle with the chocolate chips. Spread the chocolate over the hot crackers gently. Freeze for 30 minutes or until firm. Break into pieces.

Yield: 18 to 24 servings

The brook would lose its song if you removed the rocks.

Meringue Sticks with Gingered Chocolate Cream

1/2 cup confectioners' sugar, sifted

1/2 cup superfine sugar

2 tablespoons baking cocoa

3 egg whites, at room temperature

1/4 teaspoon cream of tartar

Gingered Chocolate Cream

Preheat the oven to 200 degrees. Sift the confectioners' sugar, sugar and cocoa together. Beat the egg whites and cream of tartar in a mixer bowl until soft peaks form. Add the confectioners' sugar mixture 1 tablespoon at a time, beating constantly until stiff peaks form. Spoon the meringue into a pastry tube. Pipe into 16-inch sticks 2 inches apart on a nonstick baking sheet. Bake for 1 hour. Turn off the oven. Let stand in the closed oven for 2 hours. Snap the baked meringue into 4-inch sticks. Dip into additional cocoa or sugar. May be prepared up to 5 days ahead and stored in airtight containers. Serve with Gingered Chocolate Cream.

Yield: 10 to 12 servings

Gingered Chocolate Cream

1 cup whipping cream

4 ounces semisweet chocolate, chopped

3 tablespoons minced crystallized ginger

Combine the whipping cream and chocolate in a saucepan. Cook over medium heat until the chocolate melts, stirring occasionally. Pour into a glass bowl. Cover and chill thoroughly. Beat at medium speed until thick and fluffy. Fold in the ginger. Chill, covered, until serving time.

The Pride of Brooklyn

1 pound ricotta cheese
1 pound cream cheese
1½ cups sugar
4 eggs
1 tablespoon lemon juice
3 tablespoons cornstarch
3 tablespoons flour
1 teaspoon vanilla extract
½ cup melted butter
2 cups sour cream

Preheat the oven to 325 degrees. Beat the ricotta cheese and cream cheese in a mixer bowl until light and fluffy. Add the sugar gradually, beating well after each addition. Beat in the eggs 1 at a time. Add the lemon juice, cornstarch, flour, vanilla extract and butter and beat until smooth. Blend in the sour cream. Spoon into a greased 9-inch springform pan. Bake for 1 hour. Turn off the oven. Let stand in the closed oven for 1 hour. Remove from the oven to cool completely. Chill for 6 hours to overnight before serving.

Yield: 12 to 16 servings

Triple-Chocolate Cheesecake

1/4 cup sugar

1 tablespoon margarine, softened

1 tablespoon egg white

1 1/3 cups chocolate graham cracker
  crumbs

3 tablespoons dark rum

3 ounces semisweet chocolate

1/4 cup chocolate syrup

8 ounces nonfat cream cheese,
  softened

8 ounces Neufchâtel cheese,
  softened

1 cup sugar

2 tablespoons baking cocoa

1 teaspoon vanilla extract

1/4 teaspoon salt

2 eggs

1/2 cup low-fat sour cream

1 tablespoon sugar

2 teaspoons baking cocoa

Preheat the oven to 350 degrees. Beat 1/4 cup sugar, margarine and egg white at medium speed in a mixer bowl until blended. Add the graham cracker crumbs and mix well. Press firmly over the bottom and 1 inch up the side of an 8-inch springform pan coated with nonstick cooking spray. Bake for 10 minutes. Cool on a wire rack. Reduce the oven temperature to 300 degrees. Combine the rum and chocolate in a double boiler. Cook over simmering water for 2 minutes or until the chocolate melts, stirring frequently. Remove from the heat. Add the chocolate syrup, stirring until smooth. Beat the cream cheese and Neufchâtel cheese at medium speed in a mixer bowl until smooth. Add 1 cup sugar, 2 tablespoons cocoa, vanilla extract and salt and beat well. Add the rum mixture. Beat at low speed until blended. Beat in the eggs 1 at a time. Spoon into the springform pan. Bake for 40 minutes or until almost set.

Turn off the oven. Mix the sour cream, 1 tablespoon sugar and 2 teaspoons cocoa in a bowl. Spread over the cheesecake. Let stand in the closed oven for 45 minutes. Remove from the oven to cool completely. Chill, covered, for 8 hours or longer. Garnish with chocolate curls.

♥ *Note:* See page 184 for the nutritional profile of this recipe.

Yield: 12 servings

OREO CHEESECAKE

1/4 cup finely crushed Oreo cookies

1/2 cup melted unsalted butter

1/4 cup packed light brown sugar

2 pounds cream cheese, softened

1 1/4 cups sugar

2 tablespoons flour

4 extra-large eggs

2 egg yolks

1/3 cup whipping cream

1 teaspoon vanilla extract

1 1/2 cups coarsely chopped
Oreo cookies

1 cup (about) sour cream

1/4 cup sugar

1 teaspoon vanilla extract

Swiss Fudge Glaze

5 Oreo cookies, cut into halves
crosswise

1 maraschino cherry, cut into halves

Mix 1/4 cup Oreo crumbs, butter and brown sugar in a bowl. Press over the bottom and up the side of a 9- or 10-inch springform pan. Chill for 30 minutes or until firm. Preheat the oven to 425 degrees. Beat the cream cheese at low speed in a large mixer bowl until smooth. Beat in the sugar and flour. Beat in the eggs and egg yolks 1 at a time. Stir in the whipping cream and 1 teaspoon vanilla extract. Spoon half the batter into the crust. Sprinkle with 1 1/2 cups Oreo crumbs. Top with the remaining batter, smoothing with a spatula. Bake for 15 minutes. Reduce the oven temperature to 350 degrees. Bake for 50 minutes. Cover loosely with foil if top browns too quickly. Mix the sour cream, 1/4 cup sugar and 1 teaspoon vanilla extract in a small bowl. Spread over the cheesecake. Bake for 7 minutes. Chill, covered with plastic wrap, overnight. Pour Swiss Fudge Glaze over the cheesecake, smoothing with a pastry brush.

Arrange the Oreo halves cut side down around the outer edge of the cheesecake. Place the cherry halves in the center. Chill until serving time.

Yield: 12 to 16 servings

Swiss Fudge Glaze

1 cup whipping cream

8 ounces semisweet chocolate,
chopped

1 teaspoon vanilla extract

Scald the whipping cream in a heavy medium saucepan over high heat. Add the chocolate and vanilla extract. Cook for 1 minute, stirring constantly. Remove from the heat and stir until the chocolate melts. Chill for 10 minutes.

Heavenly Cherry Angel Food Trifle

5 cups angel food cake cubes

1/4 cup cherry liqueur (optional)

1 cup confectioners' sugar

3 ounces cream cheese, softened

8 ounces whipped topping

1/2 cup toasted chopped pecans

1 (21-ounce) can cherry pie filling
   or topping

Place the cake cubes in a large bowl. Sprinkle with the liqueur. Let stand for 30 minutes. Beat the confectioners' sugar and cream cheese in a medium mixer bowl until blended. Reserve 2 tablespoons of the whipped topping. Fold the remaining whipped topping into the cream cheese mixture. Add the cream cheese mixture and pecans to the cake cubes and mix well. Spoon into an attractive glass or crystal bowl. Spread the pie filling evenly over the top. Chill, covered, for 3 hours or longer. Top each serving with a small amount of the reserved whipped topping. May instead layer the cake mixture and pie filling 1/2 at a time in the glass bowl. May substitute Grand Marnier liqueur for the cherry liqueur and 16 ounces thawed frozen strawberries or sliced fresh strawberries for the cherry pie filling.

Yield: 6 to 10 servings

*M*ANDARIN *P*RALINE *T*RIFLE

5 egg yolks

1/2 cup milk

1/2 cup sugar

1/3 cup cornstarch

2 cups milk

3/4 cup toasted sliced almonds

1 cup sugar

1/3 cup water

2/3 cup orange marmalade

1 pound cake

1/4 cup amaretto

3 (10-ounce) cans mandarin
    oranges, drained

1 1/2 cups whipping cream

For the custard, whisk the egg yolks, 1/2 cup milk, 1/2 cup sugar and cornstarch in a bowl. Heat 2 cups milk in a saucepan over medium heat until bubbles form around the edge. Whisk the hot milk gradually into the egg yolk mixture. Cook for 5 minutes or until thickened, whisking constantly. Pour into a bowl. Place plastic wrap directly on the surface of the custard. Chill for 4 hours or until completely cooled. For the pralines, arrange the almonds in a 7x9-inch rectangle on a greased baking sheet. Dissolve 1 cup sugar in 1/3 cup water in a saucepan over medium-high heat. Boil for 5 to 8 minutes or until caramel colored; do not stir. Pour over the almonds. Let cool. Break 1/3 of the praline into 5 pieces; set aside. Finely chop the remaining praline in a food processor. Press the marmalade through a sieve to measure 1/2 cup. Cut the cake into 3-inch cubes; cut each cube into halves. Spread the tops of half the cubes with marmalade. Top with the remaining cube halves, pressing together. Stand cake cubes against the side of a 12-cup glass trifle dish and cover the bottom of the dish with cake cubes. Brush with some of the amaretto. Reserve 5 orange segments. Cover the cake on the side of the bowl with half the remaining oranges. Whip 1/2 cup of the whipping cream in a mixer bowl. Fold into the custard. Fold in the chopped praline. Spread half over the oranges in the dish, leaving a border against the glass so that only the oranges show. Top with the remaining cake; brush with the remaining liqueur. Cover with the remaining oranges, then the remaining custard. Chill, covered, for 4 to 12 hours. Whip the remaining 1 cup whipping cream in a mixer bowl. Spread over the top of the trifle. Top with the reserved orange segments and reserved praline pieces.

Note: Mandarin Praline Trifle is pictured on the cover.

Yield: 12 servings

Chocolate Almond Charlotte

24 ladyfingers

1 cup orange liqueur

1 cup unsalted butter, softened

1 cup confectioners' sugar

1/4 cup orange liqueur

1 cup melted semisweet chocolate
  chips

1/4 teaspoon almond extract

1 1/2 cups ground blanched
  almonds

2 cups chilled whipping cream

Lightly butter a charlotte mold. Dip the ladyfingers 1 at a time in 1 cup liqueur. Line the side and bottom of the mold with some of the ladyfingers. Cream the butter and confectioners' sugar in a 4-quart mixer bowl until light and fluffy. Add 1/4 cup liqueur, melted chocolate and almond extract and mix gently. Add the almonds and mix gently. Beat the whipping cream in a mixer bowl until the beater leaves a small trace in the cream; do not overbeat. Fold into the chocolate mixture. Spoon 1/3 of the mixture over the ladyfingers in the mold. Add alternating layers of ladyfingers and chocolate mixture until all the ingredients are used. Cover with waxed paper; place a weighted saucer over the waxed paper. Chill for 6 hours or longer. Unmold to serve.

Yield: 12 servings

Charlotte Russe

Ladyfingers

2 tablespoons unflavored gelatin

1/4 cup cold water

2 cups scalded milk

1/2 cup sugar

4 to 6 egg yolks, beaten

1 teaspoon vanilla extract, or
   1 tablespoon brandy or other
   strong liquor

4 to 6 egg whites

1/8 teaspoon salt

2 cups whipping cream, whipped

Line a mold with ladyfingers; set aside. Soften the gelatin in the cold water. Combine with the milk in a saucepan. Cook until heated through, stirring until the gelatin is dissolved. Add the sugar, stirring until dissolved. Stir a small amount of the hot mixture into the egg yolks; stir the egg yolks into the hot mixture. Cook over very low heat until the mixture begins to thicken, stirring constantly. Let cool. Stir in the vanilla extract. Beat the egg whites and salt in a mixer bowl until stiff peaks form. Fold into the milk mixture. Fold in the whipped cream. Chill thoroughly. Unmold to serve. Serve with additional whipped cream.

Yield: 10 to 12 servings

Amaretto and Cream Cheese Flan

1/4 cup water

1 cup sugar

4 eggs

8 ounces cream cheese, softened

1 small can evaporated milk

1 can sweetened condensed milk

1/4 to 1/2 cup amaretto

Whipped cream

Preheat the oven to 350 degrees. Combine the water and sugar in a round or rectangular glass baking dish. Microwave for 5 to 7 minutes or until golden brown. Swirl the dish, coating the bottom and side with the caramel glaze. Let stand until hardened. Combine the eggs, cream cheese, evaporated milk, condensed milk and amaretto in a blender container. Process until smooth. Spoon into the prepared baking dish. Bake for 1 hour or until a wooden pick inserted near the center comes out clean. Cool on a wire rack. Unmold onto a glass plate. Chill thoroughly. Cut into wedges or slices. Top with whipped cream.

Yield: 8 to 10 servings

Cheese Torte

2 cups sugar
4 egg yolks
1 cup skim milk
2 cups grated Parmesan cheese
2 cups flour, sifted
2 teaspoons baking powder
3/4 cup melted margarine, cooled
4 egg whites, stiffly beaten
Sesame seeds

Preheat the oven to 325 degrees. Whisk the sugar, egg yolks and 1/3 cup of the skim milk in a medium bowl. Add the remaining milk and cheese alternately, whisking well after each addition. Combine the flour, baking powder and margarine in a large mixer bowl and mix until smooth. Add the cheese mixture and mix well. Fold in the egg whites. Spoon into a lightly greased and floured 9x13-inch baking pan. Sprinkle with sesame seeds. Bake for 25 to 30 minutes or until a knife inserted near the center comes out clean.

Yield: 12 servings

Peach Cobbler

3 cups sliced peaches
1 tablespoon lemon juice
1 cup self-rising flour
1 cup sugar
1 egg
1/2 cup melted margarine

Preheat the oven to 375 degrees. Place the peaches in a 1 1/2-quart baking dish. Sprinkle with the lemon juice. Mix the flour, sugar and egg in a bowl. Spread over the peaches. Pour the margarine over the top. Bake for 30 to 35 minutes or until brown and heated through. May substitute any fruit in season for the peaches.

Yield: 6 servings

ℬAKLAVA

2 pounds walnuts, coarsely chopped

1/2 cup finely crushed zwieback

1/4 cup sugar

1 teaspoon cinnamon

1/8 teaspoon nutmeg, or to taste

1/8 teaspoon allspice

1 pound phyllo dough

1 1/2 cups melted unsalted butter

2 cups water

3 cups sugar

Juice of 1/2 lemon

1 cinnamon stick

Preheat the oven to 300 degrees. Mix the walnuts, zwieback crumbs, 1/4 cup sugar, cinnamon, nutmeg and allspice in a bowl. Brush 6 to 9 phyllo sheets lightly with melted butter. Stack in a buttered 13x15-inch baking pan. Spread with some of the walnut mixture. Add lightly buttered phyllo sheets 1 layer at a time, brushing all layers except the last with some of the walnut mixture. Cut into diamond or square shapes. Bake for 1 1/2 to 2 hours or until a wooden pick inserted near the center comes out clean. Bring the water and 3 cups sugar to a boil in a saucepan. Add the lemon juice and cinnamon stick. Boil for 20 minutes. Let cool. Remove and discard the cinnamon stick. Pour the cooled syrup over the baklava.

Yield: 18 to 24 servings

Young at Heart

CHILDREN'S FAVORITES

*"That little white ball won't move until you hit it,
and there's nothing you can do after it has gone."* –Babe Zaharias

I See Children as Kites

You spend a lifetime trying to get them off the ground.

You run with them until you are both breathless,

They crash, they hit the rooftop.

You patch and comfort.

You adjust and you teach.

You watch them lifted by the wind and

Assure them that some day they'll fly.

Finally, they are airborne, and they need string

And you keep letting it all out.

But with each twist of the ball of twine

There is a sadness that goes with the joy.

The kite becomes more distant

And you know that it won't be long before that string will snap

And the lifeline that holds you together

Will no longer be the same.

A child, as a kite, must be prepared to

Soar, as they are meant to soar, free and alone,

To the greatest extent possible.

And only then can we collectively say that

We have done our job.

—Anonymous

Ian's Favorite Ranch Dip

8 ounces light cream cheese
1 cup light sour cream
1 envelope ranch salad dressing mix

Place the cream cheese in a microwave-safe bowl. Microwave on Medium for 20 to 30 seconds or until softened. Stir in the sour cream. Add the salad dressing mix, stirring until smooth and creamy. Serve immediately or chill until needed. Serve with bite-size fresh vegetables, crackers or chips.

Yield: 20 to 30 servings

Crab Dip

8 ounces cream cheese, softened
1 (6-ounce) package frozen crab meat, thawed
1/2 cup (or less) catsup
1 tablespoon chopped onion
1 tablespoon honey
1 tablespoon horseradish
1 teaspoon lemon juice

Combine the cream cheese, crab meat, catsup, onion, honey, horseradish and lemon juice in a bowl and mix well. Serve with assorted crackers and bite-size fresh vegetables.

Yield: 20 to 30 servings

Sloppy Joe Noodles

1 to 1½ pounds ground sirloin
1 large can sloppy Joe mix
3 cups water
1 small package elbow noodles

Brown the ground sirloin in a skillet, stirring until crumbly; drain well. Combine with the sloppy Joe mix in a large saucepan. Simmer over low heat until heated through. Bring the water to a boil in a medium saucepan. Add the noodles. Cook until al dente; drain. Add to the meat mixture and mix well. Simmer over low heat for 5 minutes.

Yield: 6 servings

Sean's Favorite Spaghetti Sauce

1 medium onion, chopped
1 tablespoon garlic salt
Vegetable oil
1 (28-ounce) can tomato purée
1 cup water
1 bay leaf
⅓ cup grated Romano cheese
½ cup sugar
Meatballs

Sauté the onion and garlic salt in a small amount of oil in a skillet. Add the tomato purée and water and mix well. Bring to a boil. Add the bay leaf and cheese and mix well. Simmer for several minutes. Add the sugar and test for taste; the sauce should be only slightly sweet. Boil for 5 minutes; reduce the heat. Simmer, covered, for 15 minutes. Cook over low heat for 3 hours, stirring every 15 minutes and adding the meatballs during the last 45 minutes cooking time. Remove and discard the bay leaf before serving.

Yield: 8 to 10 servings

Meat Loaf Your Children Will Eat

1 egg, lightly beaten
1 pound ground round
8 ounces ground pork
1/2 cup cracker crumbs
1 small onion, chopped
1 tablespoon horseradish
1 tablespoon catsup
1 tablespoon chopped green
    bell pepper
1 teaspoon salt
1 teaspoon sugar
1 cup scalded milk
Chopped basil, marjoram and
    parsley

Preheat the oven to 350 degrees. Combine the egg, ground round, ground pork, cracker crumbs, onion, horseradish, catsup, green pepper, salt and sugar in a bowl and mix well. Add the milk and mix well. Shape into a loaf in a loaf pan. Top with basil, marjoram and parsley. Bake for 1 hour. May substitute other favorite seasonings for basil, marjoram and parsley.

Yield: 8 servings

The greater the obstacle, the more glory in overcoming it.

—Molière

CRITTER CUPCAKES

Your favorite cupcakes, baked,
  cooled
1 can prepared white icing
Large marshmallows
Miniature marshmallows
Andes mint candies
Miniature jelly beans
Fruit strings candy
Gumdrops
Candy peanuts
Little Debbie Swiss cake rolls
Baking cocoa
Food coloring

You won't need all the ingredients listed at the left unless you're making each variety of Critter Cupcakes. So read through the recipes first before you do the shopping. The recipes that follow are given for 1 cupcake each.

Note: Critter Cupcakes are pictured on the cover.

Dog Cupcake

Baking cocoa
2 tablespoons icing
2 Andes mint candies (ears)
2 miniature marshmallows (snout)
1 brown jelly bean (nose)
1 red jelly bean (tongue)
2 blue jelly beans (eyes)

Stir enough cocoa into the icing to make it brown. Spread over the cupcake. Round off the bottom corners of the mints; cut the tops into triangles. Press onto the sides of the cupcake for the ears. Press the marshmallows into the center of the cupcake. Press in the brown jelly bean where the marshmallows meet to make a nose. Lay the red jelly bean flat for the tongue. Press the blue jelly beans in above the marshmallows for the eyes.

Bear Cupcake

Baking cocoa
2 tablespoons icing
1 Swiss cake roll (ears)
1 large marshmallow (snout)
1 black jelly bean (nose)
2 brown jelly beans (eyes)

Stir enough cocoa into the icing to make it brown. Set aside a small amount of icing. Spread the remaining icing over the cupcake. Cut two ¹/₂-inch slices from the Swiss cake; press onto the sides of the cupcake for the ears. Press the marshmallow onto the lower center of the cupcake for the snout. Place the reserved icing on the black jelly bean; lay the jelly bean horizontally over the snout for the nose. Press the brown jelly beans in above the snout for the eyes.

Elephant Cupcake

2 tablespoons icing, tinted purple
2 purple gumdrops (ears)
1 purple gumdrop, stretched, or
*   1 candy peanut (trunk)*
2 green jelly beans (eyes)

Spread the cupcake with icing. Flatten the ear gumdrops and press one on each side of the cupcake. Place the stretched gumdrop in the center of the cupcake, pointing down, for the trunk. Place 1 jelly bean on each side of the trunk for the eyes.

continued on page 174

You can never do a kindness too soon because you never know how soon it will be too late.

–Ralph Waldo Emerson

Pig Cupcake

3 tablespoons icing, tinted pink
1 large marshmallow (snout)
2 Andes mint candies (ears)
2 blue jelly beans (eyes)
2 brown jelly beans (nostrils)

Spread the cupcake with most of the icing. Press the marshmallow into the lower center of the cupcake; spread the marshmallow with a small amount of icing. Cut 1 triangle from each candy; press onto the sides of the cupcake for the ears. Press the blue jelly beans into the cupcake above the snout for the eyes. Lay the brown jelly beans parallel to each other over the snout for the nostrils.

Cat Cupcake

2 tablespoons icing, tinted orange
2 Andes mint candies (ears)
2 miniature marshmallows (snout)
1 pink jelly bean (nose)
2 green jelly beans (eyes)
Fruit strings candy, or Andes mint candies cut into long thin strips (whiskers)

Spread the cupcake with icing. Cut 1 triangle from each candy; press onto the sides of the cupcake for the ears. Press the marshmallows into the lower center of the cupcake for the snout. Press the pink jelly bean above the intersection of the marshmallows for the nose. Press the green jelly beans into the icing for the eyes. Press the string candy into the icing on both sides of the snout for the whiskers.

Porcupine Cupcake

Baking cocoa
2 tablespoons icing
1 brown gumdrop (snout)
1 black jelly bean (nose)
1 red jelly bean (mouth)
2 blue jelly beans (eyes)
4 Andes mint candies, cut into short strips (quills)

Stir enough cocoa into the icing to make it brown. Spread most of the icing over the cupcake. Press the gumdrop into the lower center of the cupcake for the snout. Dip the back of the black jelly bean into the remaining icing; attach to the end of the snout for the nose. Place the red jelly bean just below the snout for the mouth. Press the blue jelly beans into the icing for the eyes. Insert the candy strips in a circular pattern all around the face for the quills.

Bird Nest Treats

1/4 cup butter or margarine

4 1/2 cups miniature marshmallows

1/4 cup creamy peanut butter

1/4 cup semisweet chocolate chips

4 cups chow mein noodles

1 cup jelly beans or candy eggs

Melt the butter and marsh-mallows in a large saucepan over medium heat, stirring occasionally until blended and smooth. Add the peanut butter and chocolate chips. Cook for 2 minutes, stirring constantly. Remove from the heat. Add the noodles, stirring until coated. Divide the mixture into 12 mounds on a waxed-paper-lined baking sheet. Shape each mound into a "nest." Press an indentation into the center of each nest. Fill each nest with 3 or 4 jelly beans. Let cool. Store in an airtight container.

Yield: 1 dozen

Man is a creature of hope and invention, both of which belie the idea that things cannot be changed.

–Tom Clancy

Puppy Chow (Just for Kids)

1/4 cup margarine or butter
1 large package chocolate chips
1 cup creamy peanut butter
1 package Crispix or rice Chex
  cereal
1 (1-pound) package confectioners'
  sugar

Combine the margarine, chocolate chips and peanut butter in a microwave-safe bowl. Microwave until melted, stirring occasionally until blended and smooth. Combine with the cereal in a large bowl and mix well. Pour into a large zip-top plastic bag. Add the confectioners' sugar, shaking or stirring until coated.

Yield: 30 to 40 servings

Healthy Initial Crackers

1 1/2 cups self-rising flour
1/8 tablespoon garlic salt, or
  to taste
2 tablespoons sesame seeds
3 tablespoons cold margarine
2 tablespoons ice water

Preheat the oven to 350 degrees. Combine the flour, garlic salt, sesame seeds and margarine in a bowl and mix until crumbly. Add the ice water and mix well. Shape into a ball. Pinch off small amounts of the dough at a time and shape into thin strips. Shape into desired initials. Place on a cookie sheet sprayed with nonstick cooking spray. Bake for 15 minutes.

Yield: 8 to 10 servings

I do not ask to walk

smooth paths

Nor bear an easy load.

I pray for strength

and fortitude

To climb the

rock-strewn road.

Give me such courage

I can scale

The hardest peaks alone,

And transform every

stumbling block

Into a stepping stone.

—Gail Burkett

Arabian Hats

1 3/4 cups flour

1 teaspoon baking soda

1/2 teaspoon salt

1/2 cup sugar

1/2 cup packed brown sugar

1/2 cup butter-flavor shortening

1/2 cup peanut butter

1 egg

2 tablespoons milk

1 teaspoon vanilla extract

Sugar

48 chocolate candy kisses

Preheat the oven to 350 degrees. Combine the flour, baking soda, salt, 1/2 cup sugar, brown sugar, shortening, peanut butter, egg, milk and vanilla extract in a large bowl. Mix well until a soft dough forms. Shape into balls slightly larger than a quarter. Roll in additional sugar. Place on a nonstick cookie sheet. Press a candy kiss into each cookie firmly enough that the cookies crack around the edge. Bake for 10 to 12 minutes or until light brown.

Yield: 4 dozen

Miniature Elephant Ears

1 (10-count) package frozen dinner
    rolls, thawed

Vegetable oil

3 tablespoons melted butter or
    margarine

1/2 cup sugar

1 tablespoon cinnamon

Stretch each piece of dough into a flat ear shape. Fry a few pieces at a time in hot oil in an electric skillet or deep fryer for 1 1/2 minutes per side or until brown; drain well. Brush with butter. Sprinkle with a mixture of sugar and cinnamon.

Yield: 10 servings

POPSICLES

1 (3-ounce) package any flavor
  gelatin
1 envelope any flavor drink mix
1 cup sugar
1 cup boiling water
3 cups cold water

Combine the gelatin, drink mix, sugar, boiling water and cold water in a bowl and mix well. Pour into popsicle molds with handles. Freeze until firm.

Yield: 6 servings

FUDGESICLES

1 (4-ounce) package chocolate
  instant pudding mix
2 cups milk
1/4 cup sugar

Combine the pudding mix, milk and sugar in a bowl and mix well. Pour into popsicle molds with handles. Freeze until firm.

Yield: 6 servings

I know not the way
I'm going but
Well do I know my Guide.
With a child's faith do
I give my hand
To the mighty friend
by my side.
And the only thing I say to
Him as he takes it
Is, "Hold it fast!"
Suffer me not to lose the
way and lead me
Home at last.

Krispie Peanut Butter Balls

1½ cups creamy peanut butter or low-fat creamy peanut butter

½ to ¾ cup nonfat dry milk powder

½ cup honey

3 to 4 cups (or more) Cocoa Krispies cereal

Combine the peanut butter, dry milk powder and honey in a large bowl and mix well. Add 1 to 1½ cups of the cereal and mix well. Place the remaining cereal in another bowl. Spray hands and fingers lightly with nonstick cooking spray; repeat spraying as needed. Roll a nickel-size piece of the peanut butter mixture into a ball. Drop the ball into the cereal, rolling it around until coated. Place on a nonstick cookie sheet; do not spray or grease the cookie sheet. Repeat with the remaining ingredients. Chill for 30 minutes. Remove to a decorative platter to serve.

Leftovers may be stored, covered, in the refrigerator for several days. May add 1 tablespoon or more malted milk powder, roll in finely crushed unsalted peanuts, roll in wheat germ, wrap the peanut butter mixture around miniature marshmallows, or dip the balls into melted chocolate.

Yield: 1 dozen

Peanut Butter Oatmeal Cookies

1 cup peanut butter
1/2 cup margarine, softened
1 cup packed brown sugar
2 eggs
1 teaspoon vanilla extract
1 teaspoon baking soda
1 cup rolled oats
2 cups flour

Preheat the oven to 350 degrees. Combine the peanut butter, margarine and brown sugar in a bowl and mix until smooth. Add the eggs, vanilla extract and baking soda and mix well. Add the oats and flour and mix well. Drop by teaspoonfuls onto a nonstick cookie sheet. Bake for 13 minutes. Cool on the cookie sheet for 5 minutes. Remove to a wire rack to cool completely.

Yield: 3 dozen

Aunt Fannie's Fruitcake Cups

1/2 pound candied cherries, finely chopped
1/4 pound candied pineapple, finely chopped
1 cup flour
1 can sweetened condensed milk
3/4 cup melted butter
4 cups chopped pecans

Preheat the oven to 325 degrees. Combine the cherries, pineapple, flour, condensed milk, butter and pecans in a bowl and mix well. Drop by spoonfuls into miniature muffin cups. Bake for 20 minutes.

Yield: 5 dozen

DIRT CAKE

2 small packages French vanilla
   instant pudding mix
3 cups milk
8 ounces cream cheese, softened
1/2 cup margarine, softened
12 ounces whipped topping
4 tablespoons confectioners' sugar
2 packages Oreo cookies, crushed
Gummy worms (optional)

Wash a new 7-inch clay flowerpot and let dry. Blend the pudding mix and milk in a medium bowl and set aside. Combine the cream cheese, margarine, whipped topping and confectioners' sugar in a large bowl and mix well. Blend in the pudding mixture. Alternate layers of the cookie crumbs and cream cheese mixture in the flowerpot, ending with 1 inch of cookie crumbs. Insert a plastic plant or flowers into the center. Press the gummy worms partially into the top.

Yield: 15 servings

I saw one walk with Courage, hand in hand—
So young and frail, I could not understand
The quiet serenity with which he bore
So high and steadily, a weight so sore;
Til following him along the road he trod,
I saw that Courage wore the face of God.

Oreo Turkey Treats

1 (16-ounce) package Oreos
1/4 cup red cinnamon candies
1 1/4 cups malted milk balls
1 (16-ounce) can ready-to-spread
    chocolate frosting
1 (9-ounce) package candy corn

Separate each cookie carefully, leaving the cream filling intact on 1 side (this will be the base for the turkey); set aside. To make the turkey body, attach a cinnamon candy (head) to each malted milk ball (body) with a dab of frosting. Spread frosting over the inside of each cookie half that does not have the cream filling. For the turkey tail, arrange candy corn on the frosting on the cookie halves, with the wide end of the candy along the outer edge. Attach each turkey tail behind each body with frosting. Attach a turkey body to the center of each cream-filled cookie half with a dab of frosting.

Note: Oreo Turkey Treats are pictured on the cover.

Yield: 42 servings

Tenderheart Tarts

1/2 cup honey
1 cup creamy peanut butter
1 1/4 cups dry milk powder
Raspberry jam

Pour the honey over the peanut butter in a bowl and mix well. Add the dry milk powder and mix until a soft dough forms. Shape into large marble-sized balls. Press into rounds on a wooden board. Shape each round into a heart. Place a dab of jam in the center of each heart. Arrange on a plate. Chill for 1 hour or longer.

Yield: 30 servings.

Piña Colada Wedges

8 ounces cream cheese, softened

1/3 cup sugar

1/2 teaspoon rum extract

3 1/2 cups whipped topping

1 (8-ounce) can crushed pineapple
  in syrup

2 2/3 cups shredded coconut

Line an 8-inch round pan with plastic wrap. Beat the cream cheese, sugar and rum extract in a bowl until smooth. Fold in 2 cups of the whipped topping, undrained pineapple and 2 cups of the coconut. Spread in the prepared pan. Invert onto a freezer-proof serving plate. Remove the pan and the plastic wrap. Spread with the remaining whipped topping. Sprinkle with the remaining coconut. Freeze for 2 hours or until firm. Cut into wedges to serve. Garnish with pineapple chunks and cherries.

Yield: 8 to 12 servings

Children can learn to live with a disability. But they cannot live well without the connection that their parents find them utterly lovable. When something is wrong with a child, he needs to be certain it does not interfere with his parents' love for him.

—Bruno Bettelheim

Nutritional Profiles

We have attempted to present these family recipes in a format that allows approximate nutritional values to be computed. Persons with dietary or health problems or whose diets require close monitoring should not rely solely on the nutritional information provided. They should consult their physicians or a registered dietitian for specific information.

Nutritional Profile Abbreviations

Cal – Calories
Prot – Protein
Carbo – Carbohydrates
T Fat – Total Fat
Chol – Cholesterol
Fiber – Dietary Fiber
Sod – Sodium
g – grams
mg – milligrams

Nutritional information is computed from information derived from many sources, including materials supplied by the United States Department of Agriculture, computer databanks and journals in which the information is assumed to be in the public domain. However, many specialty items, new products and processed foods may not be available from these sources or may vary from the average values used in these profiles. More information on new and/or specific products may be obtained by reading the nutrient labels. Unless specified, the nutritional profile of these recipes is based on all measurements being level.

- **Artificial sweeteners** vary in use and strength so should be used "to taste," using the recipe ingredients as a guideline. Sweeteners using aspartame (NutraSweet and Equal) should not be used as a sweetener in recipes involving prolonged heating, which reduces the sweet taste. For further information on the use of these sweeteners, refer to the package.
- **Alcoholic ingredients** have been analyzed for the basic ingredients, although cooking causes the evaporation of alcohol, thus decreasing caloric content.
- **Buttermilk**, **sour cream**, and **yogurt** are commercial types.
- **Cake mixes** that are prepared using package directions include 3 eggs and 1/2 cup oil.

- **Chicken**, cooked for boning and chopping, has been roasted.
- **Cottage cheese** is cream-style with 4.2% creaming mixture. Dry curd cottage cheese has no creaming mixture.
- **Eggs** are all large. To avoid raw eggs that may carry salmonella, as in eggnog or 6-week muffin batter, use an equivalent amount of commercial egg substitute.
- **Flour** is unsifted all-purpose flour.
- **Garnishes**, serving suggestions, optional information, and variations are not included.
- **Margarine** and **butter** are regular, not whipped or presoftened.
- **Milk** is whole milk, 3.5% butterfat. Low-fat milk is 1% butterfat. Evaporated milk is whole milk with 60% of the water removed.
- **Oil** is any type of vegetable cooking oil. **Shortening** is hydrogenated vegetable shortening.
- **Salt** and other ingredients to taste as noted in the ingredients are not included in the profile.
- If a choice of ingredients is given, the profile reflects the first option. If a choice of amounts is given, the profile reflects the greater amount.

$\mathscr{N}$UTRITIONAL $\mathscr{P}$ROFILES

Pg. No.	Recipe Title (Approx Per Serving)	Cal	Prot (g)	Carbo (g)	T Fat (g)	% Cal from Fat	Chol (mg)	Fiber (g)	Sod (mg)
39	Oatmeal Bread	143	4	29	1	9	0	1	304
66	Asian Chicken Salad	109	15	7	2	14	38	1	366
68	Heart-Smart Crab Salad	154	18	12	3	20	50	2	331
80	Grilled Marinated Pork with Sweet Mustard Sauce	331	26	29	13	34	67	1	659
87	Chicken Brochettes with Red Bell Pepper and Feta Cheese	179	26	7	5	25	72	1	190
88	Crunchy Salsa Chicken	300	38	25	6	18	73	6	218
89	Chicken Fajitas from the East	319	8	56	7	21	<1	5	558
90	Stir-Fried Chicken with Raspberry Vinegar	183	18	14	5	26	42	2	237
93	Turkey Mexique	184	24	9	6	30	53	2	483
93	Rosemary and Garlic Turkey	146	23	7	2	15	63	<1	88
97	Sweet-and-Sour Fish Steaks	156	16	12	4	25	30	1	75
99	Grilled Salmon Steaks with Cantaloupe Salsa	371	34	9	22	54	102	1	743
102	Parchment Shrimp	231	35	6	7	28	257	2	736
106	Tuna Steaks Glazed with Ginger, Lime and Soy Sauce	281	41	3	10	34	67	<1	259
108	Mexican Spaghetti	331	27	43	6	15	42	4	1040
109	Seafood Pasta	558	54	66	7	12	152	4	1042
114	Pasta and Vegetables with Peanut Sauce	306	10	53	7	19	<1	4	409
115	Mediterranean Orzo	161	5	25	4	24	6	2	204
118	Lentil Spaghetti Sauce	180	12	25	5	23	3	12	92
149	One-Bowl Low-Fat Brownies	232	4	45	6	21	<1	2	27
158	Triple-Chocolate Cheesecake	300	8	41	12	34	55	1	331

Index

For additional copies of

send:
$19.95 plus $4.95 postage and handling
(Georgia residents include 7% sales tax)
for each book

to:
Children's Heart Program Volunteer Council
Medical College of Georgia Children's Medical Center
1120 15th Street / BAA 800W
Augusta, Georgia 30912

or:
call 706-721-COOK.

Make checks payable to Children's Heart Program, MCG Foundation.

𝒩OTES

New Hope for Children with Heart Disease

About eight in every thousand children—about 25,000 infants per year in the United States—will be born with a heart defect. An additional 40,000 children aged one or older are diagnosed with heart problems. It is comforting to know that today we can have more confidence than ever about what the future holds for our children with heart disease. Some congenital heart defects repair themselves, some require medication and medical management and others need surgical correction.

Thousands of adults are alive today only because of the advances in diagnosing and treating heart disease over the past 50 years. Today is an exciting and hopeful time for children with heart defects; their chances of living normal and active lives are greatly enhanced since most congenital heart defects can be corrected in infancy or early childhood.

Advanced technology in pediatric cardiology has opened new avenues in treating children with heart defects. Children with heart disease differ vastly from adult heart patients. While adults typically have coronary artery problems in otherwise normal hearts, children have structural defects. Because children are not just small adults, medical technology has been specifically designed for children. Previously, technology used for adults was just scaled down to a smaller size. Dedicated programs like the Children's Heart Program at the Medical College of Georgia Children's Medical Center provide unique and distinct programs to help our children manage or treat heart disease, offer hope for future generations through scientific research and prevent healthy children from getting heart disease.

Three groups comprise the Children's Heart Program at the Medical College of Georgia Children's Medical Center. The Children's Heart Group encompasses the clinical arm of the Children's Heart Program and is the team of all disciplines related to children with heart abnormalities and their families. The group maintains satellite offices in Georgia cities so pediatric cardiologists can evaluate children with suspected heart disease. The Heart Development Group at the Medical College of Georgia is recognized internationally for new findings in heart development research. The group explores aspects of heart development and studies the source of heart defects. Their findings put us one step closer to preventing congenital heart disease. The Cardiac Studies Group at the Prevention Institute at the Medical College of Georgia is also internationally known for its research in identifying children at greatest risk for developing cardiovascular diseases as adults. This group conducts clinical research and emphasizes heart-healthy lifestyles.

The Children's Heart Program Volunteer Council embraces the efforts of these three groups.